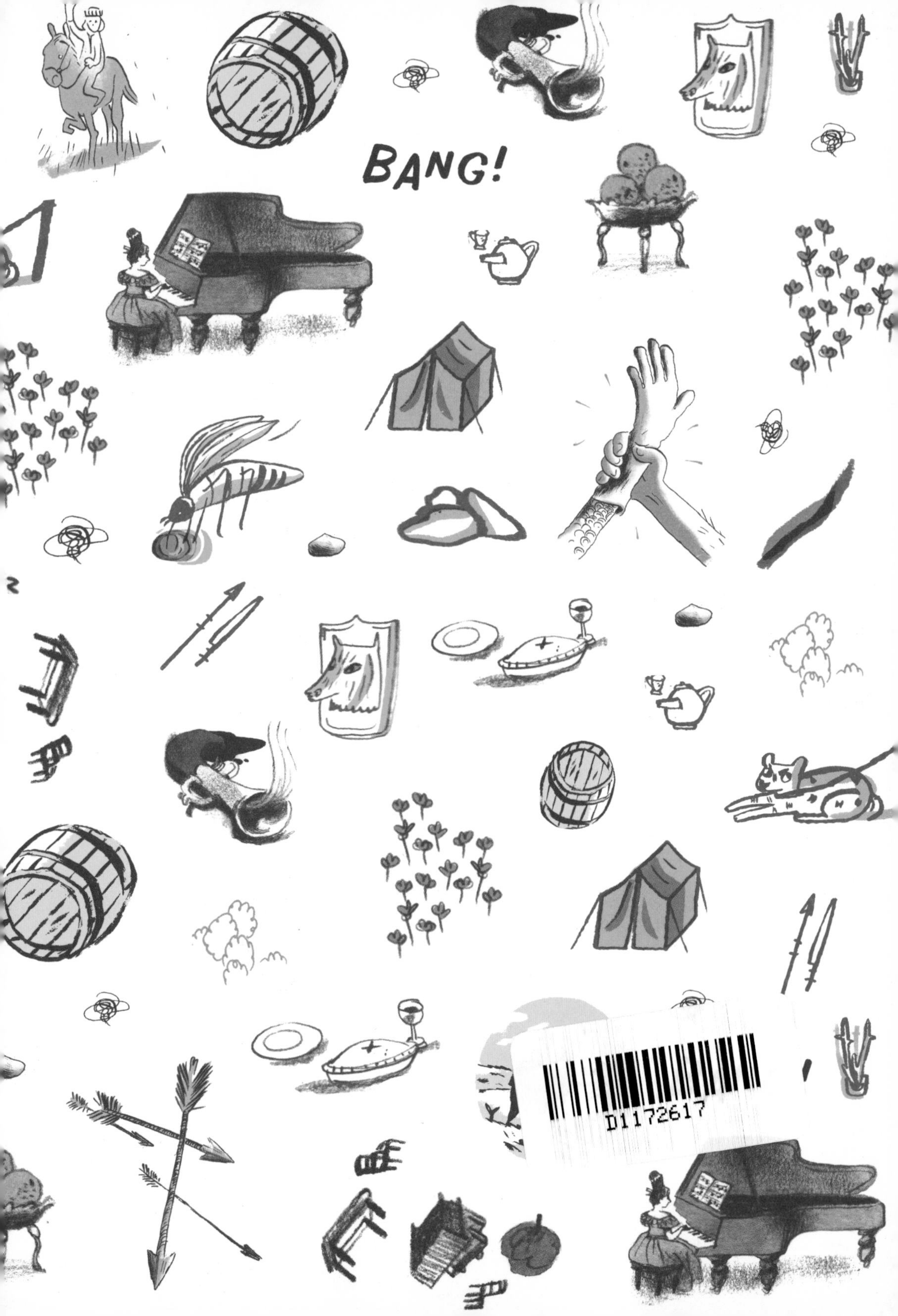
BANG!

A Castle in England © Nobrow 2017.

A collaboration with Scotney Castle and the National Trust.
Supported by the Arts Council England.

This is a first edition published in 2017 by Nobrow Ltd. 27 Westgate Street, London E8 3RL.

Text © Jamie Rhodes 2017. Illustrations © Isaac Lenkiewicz, Briony May Smith, William Exley, Becky Palmer, and Isabel Greenberg 2017. Cover illustration © William Exley.

Jamie Rhodes, Isaac Lenkiewicz, Briony May Smith, William Exley, Becky Palmer, and Isabel Greenberg have asserted their right under the Copyright, Designs and Patents Act, 1988, to be identified as the Author and Illustrators of this Work.

Published in the US by Nobrow (US) Inc.
Printed in Latvia on FSC® certified paper.

ISBN: 978-1-910620-19-9

Order from www.nobrow.net

FSC
www.fsc.org

MIX
Paper from
responsible sources
FSC® C002795

a castle in england

written by Jamie Rhodes

NOBROW
LONDON | NEW YORK

PREFACE

Castles mature over time. Centuries of human interaction etched into every stone, staining every beam, every floorboard trodden by a thousand footsteps, trodden by feet long dead.

Each castle is a piece of art wrought from its own unique brushstrokes of smiles and tears, struggles, victories, business deals, marriages, subterfuge, births, and deaths. Extraordinary or mundane, the castle bears witness to everything; it is the stage on which endless stories play out. Stories of humans, animals, and indeed the landscape itself. From the whispers of lovers to the screams of the murdered, from the merriment of dancers to the whimpers of the frightened. The deer on the grounds, the fish in the moat, the blades of grass reaching up through the cold earth. Lives come and go, but the castle remains.

Next time you visit a castle, pause outside for a moment and feel the enormous weight of history before you. Appreciate the castle for all its complexity. Though it may be beautiful, that beauty is not simply in the building as made by an architect. Feel moved by what you see as an incidental collective work of art, ripe with an infinite number of stories spun out by a chaotic universe, to convene upon this one point, beheld by you for this one moment. Then step inside.

From January to April 2016, I had the honour of living on-site at Scotney Castle in Kent, South-East England, whilst I researched and wrote these stories. I worked with the staff and volunteers to look through the castle's vast unexplored archive and collection, discovering as much as I could about the people that lived there and events that took place.

I walked the ancient holloways through the grounds, I sat amongst the old castle ruins as I wrote, and even had a favourite armchair in the library of the Victorian mansion. The castle is cared for by the National Trust and I had the privilege of learning from their experts. It is always a thrill to learn from someone who is an expert in their field, I can't thank them enough for giving me their time.

It was an incredible experience and one I will carry with me forever.

As you might imagine, I struggled to choose only five stories for this book. Many were left out and I could have written many more. In the end I went for stories which offered a broad spread of the castle's history, with characters created for five different centuries, all inspired by those seeds of inspiration found through working with the staff and immersing myself in the world of the castle.

Castles throughout the world are deep wells of stories and I hope to explore more someday. For now, I am proud to offer you five from A Castle in England.

— Jamie Rhodes

National
Trust

LOTTERY FUNDED

Supported using public funding by

ARTS COUNCIL
ENGLAND

De Scotenie Family Tree
Built the original castle

—

From the Middle ages and the Medieval Era

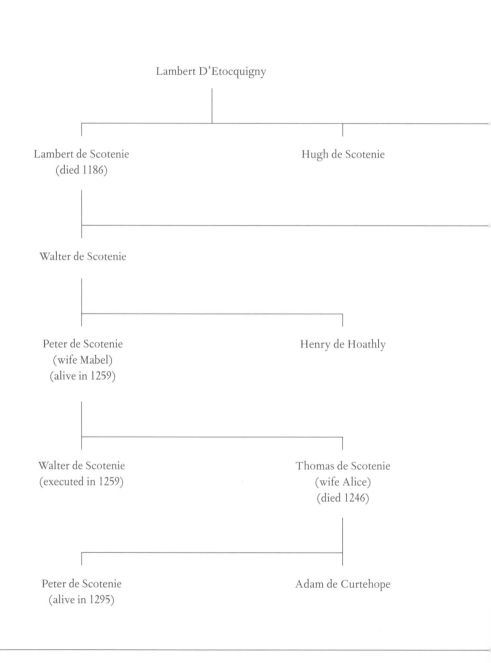

Lambert D'Etocquigny

Lambert de Scotenie
(died 1186)

Hugh de Scotenie

Walter de Scotenie

Peter de Scotenie
(wife Mabel)
(alive in 1259)

Henry de Hoathly

Walter de Scotenie
(executed in 1259)

Thomas de Scotenie
(wife Alice)
(died 1246)

Peter de Scotenie
(alive in 1295)

Adam de Curtehope

NOTE:

This information has been derived from various early documents and we cannot be sure of the accuracy

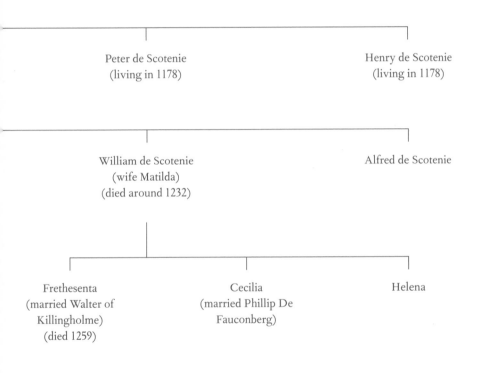

Peter de Scotenie
(living in 1178)

Henry de Scotenie
(living in 1178)

William de Scotenie
(wife Matilda)
(died around 1232)

Alfred de Scotenie

Frethesenta
(married Walter of Killingholme)
(died 1259)

Cecilia
(married Phillip De Fauconberg)

Helena

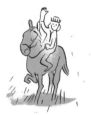

THE LABOURER

by Isaac Lenkiewicz

A fourteen year-old boy, King Richard II of the House Plantagenet, rules the Kingdom of England. To pay for the costly war with France, his advisors have been imposing unsustainable taxes on an already impoverished population of "unfree" serfs. The peasant labourers building Scotney Castle are no exception. But the common people can only be pushed so far, before a spark ignites the powder keg and bloody revolution rips through the country…

Medieval Era
The Peasant's Revolt
- 1381 -

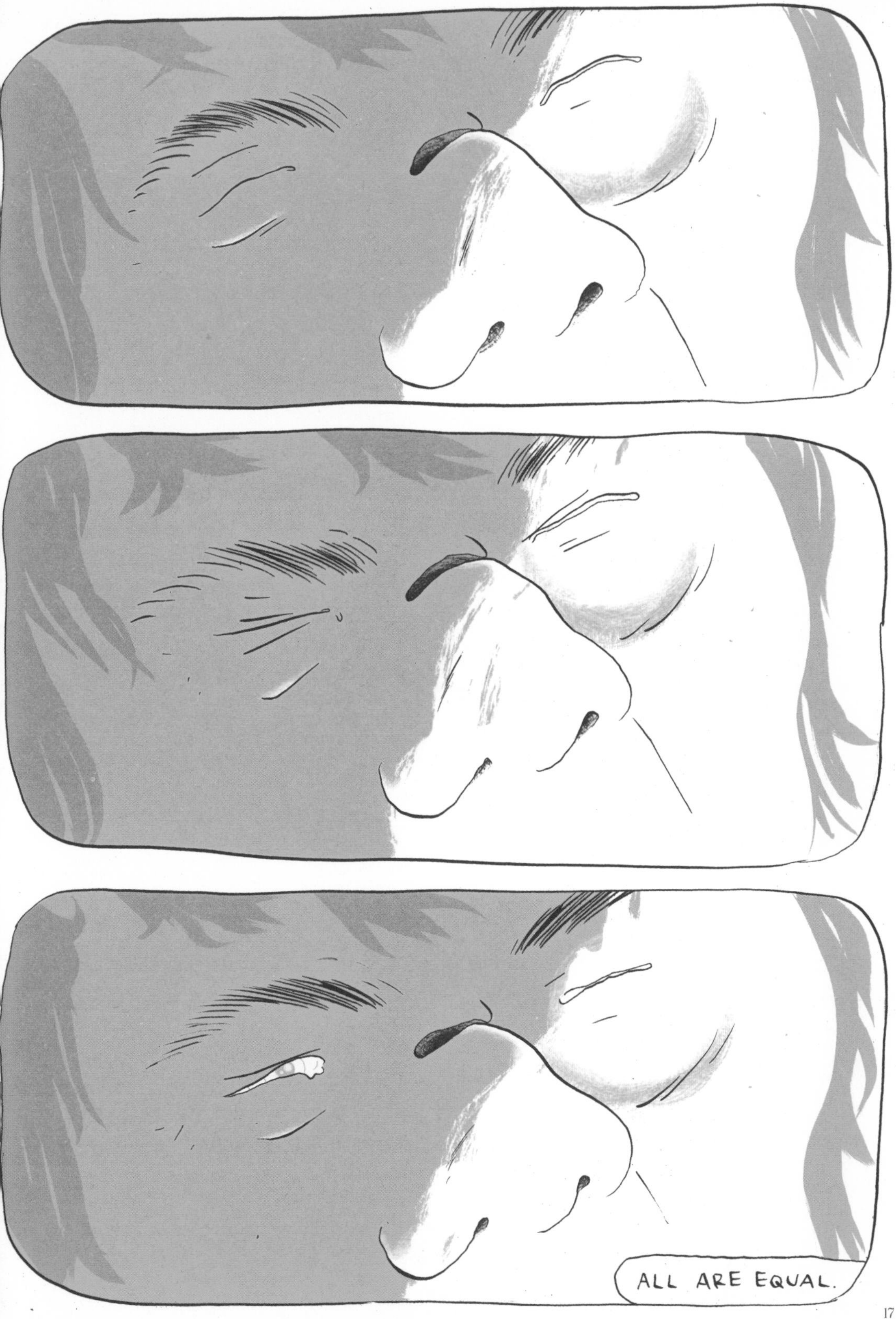
ALL ARE EQUAL.

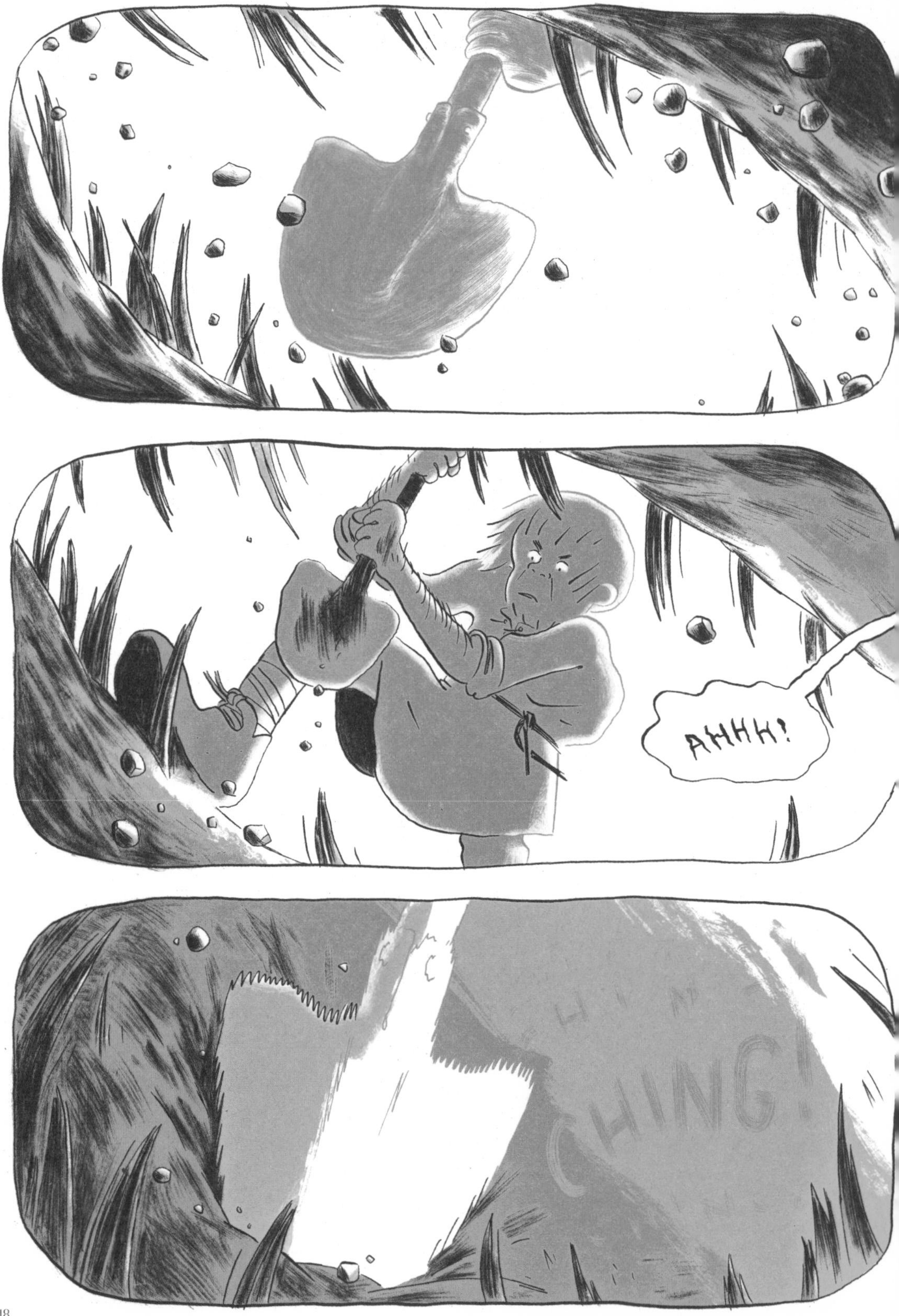
AHHH!
CHING!

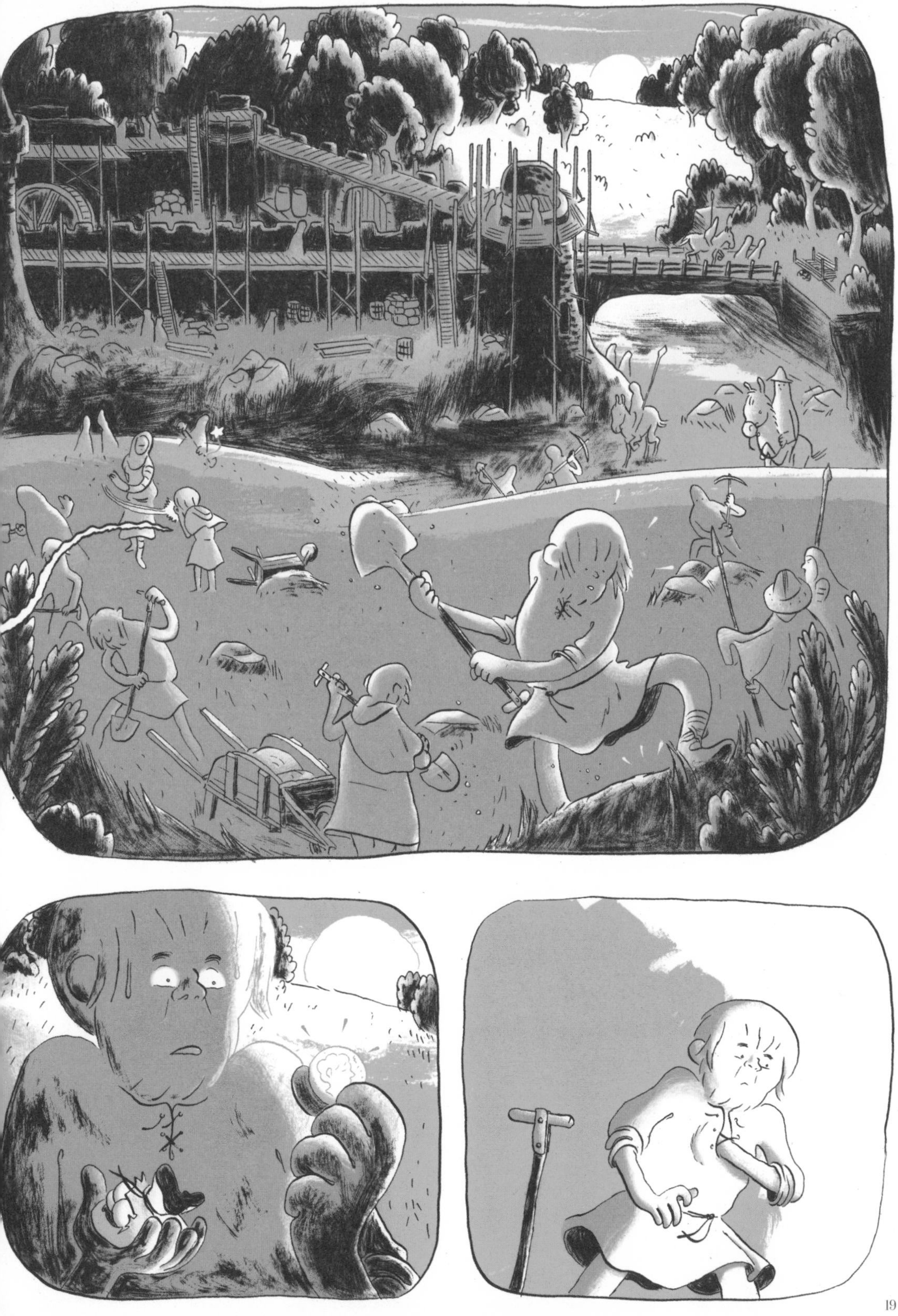

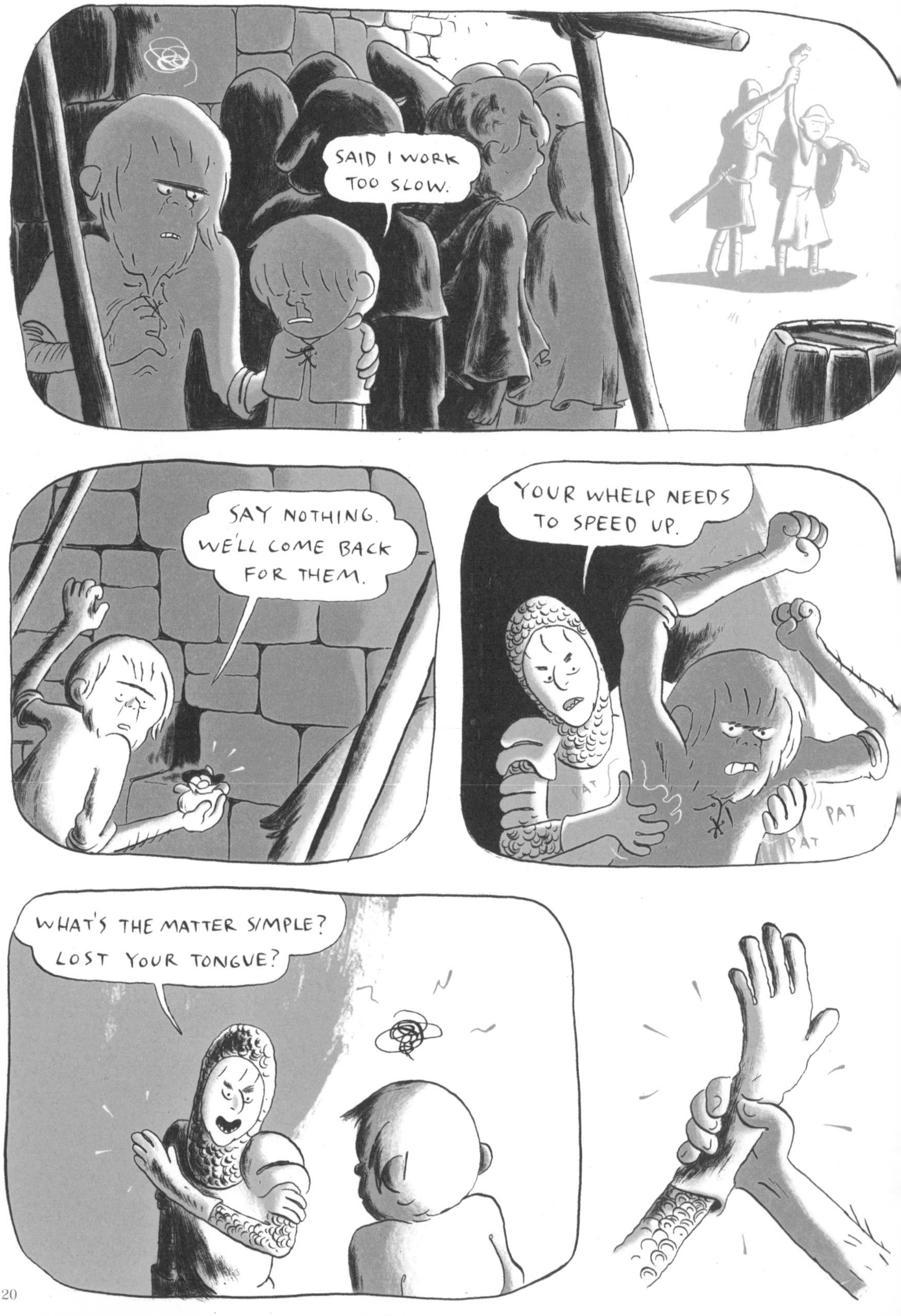
SAID I WORK TOO SLOW.
SAY NOTHING. WE'LL COME BACK FOR THEM.
YOUR WHELP NEEDS TO SPEED UP.
PAT
PAT
PAT
WHAT'S THE MATTER SIMPLE? LOST YOUR TONGUE?

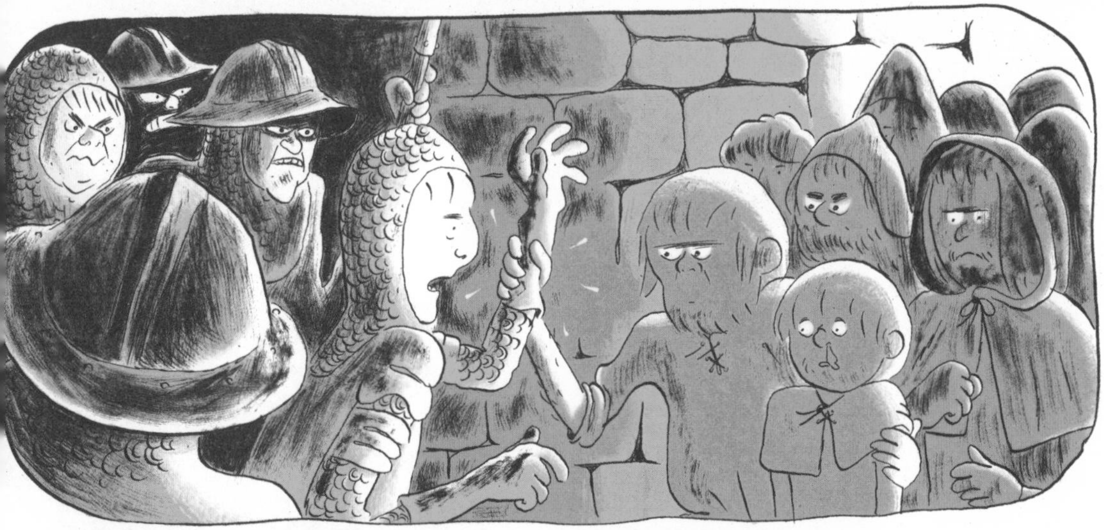

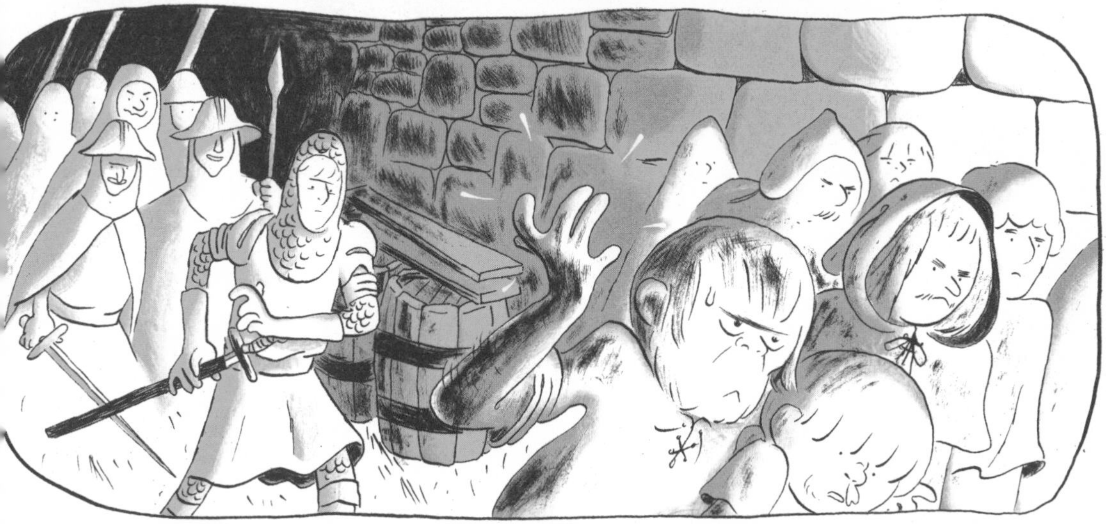

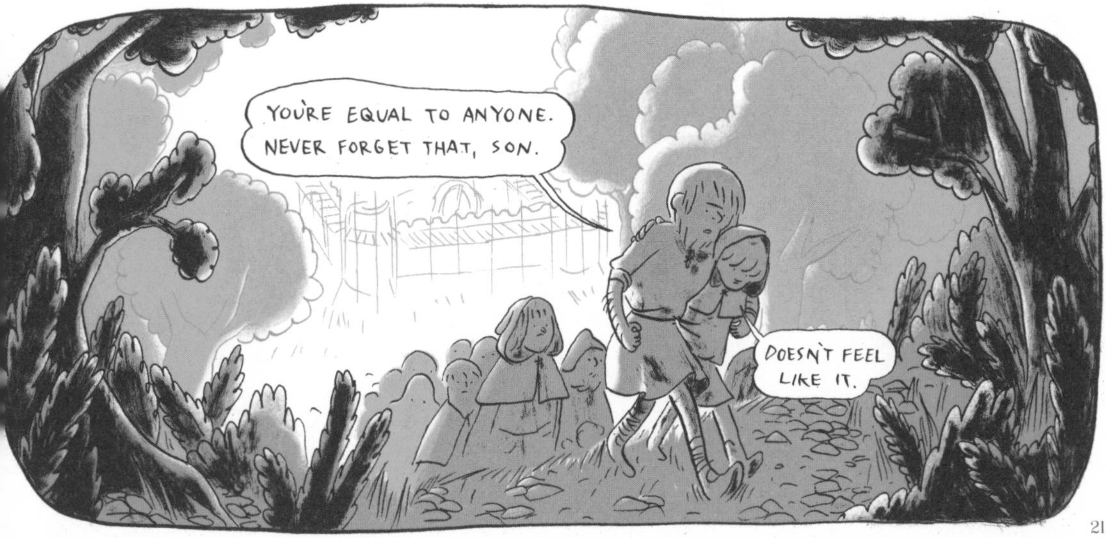
YOU'RE EQUAL TO ANYONE. NEVER FORGET THAT, SON.
DOESN'T FEEL LIKE IT.

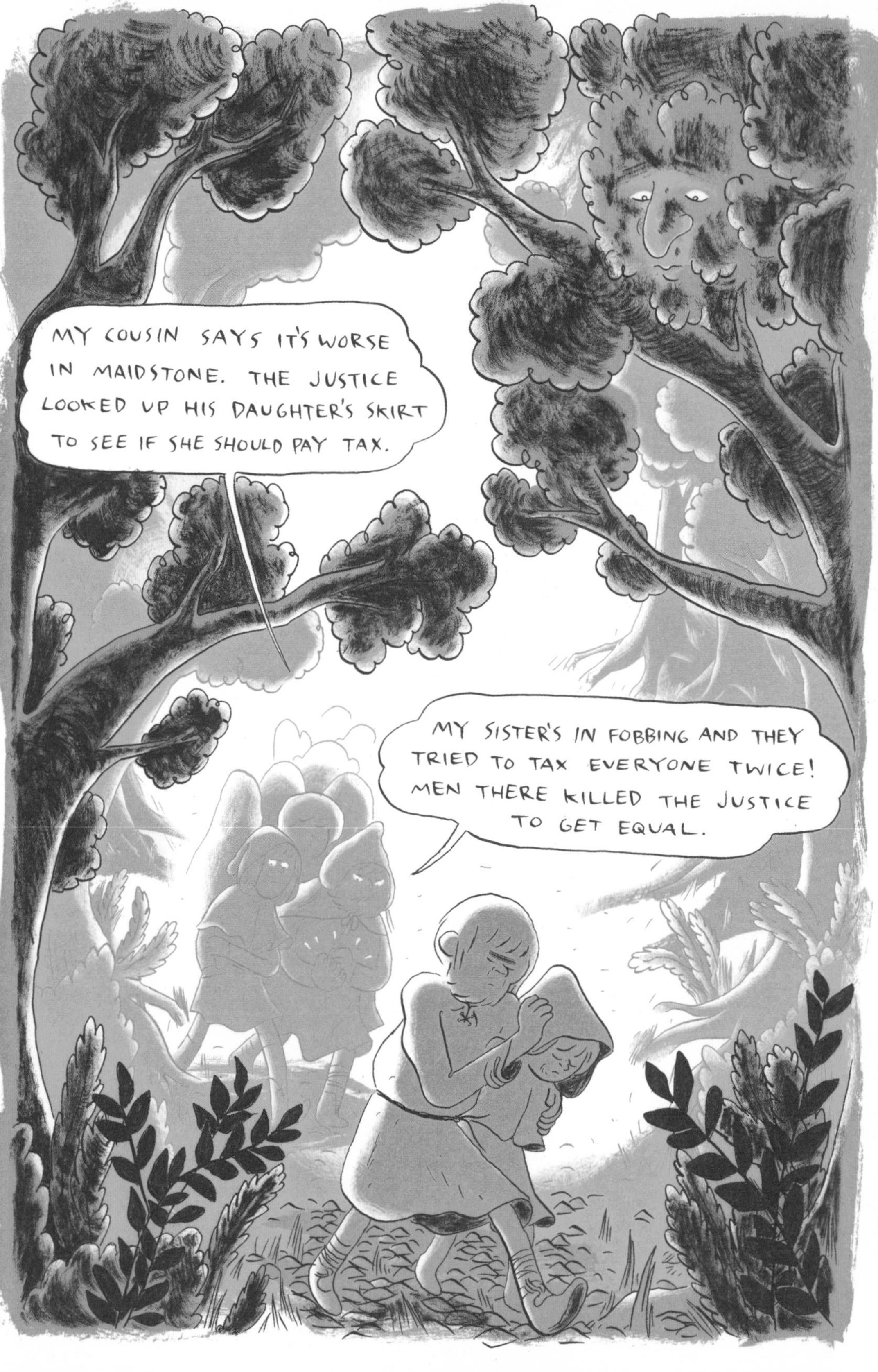
MY COUSIN SAYS IT'S WORSE IN MAIDSTONE. THE JUSTICE LOOKED UP HIS DAUGHTER'S SKIRT TO SEE IF SHE SHOULD PAY TAX.
MY SISTER'S IN FOBBING AND THEY TRIED TO TAX EVERYONE TWICE! MEN THERE KILLED THE JUSTICE TO GET EQUAL.

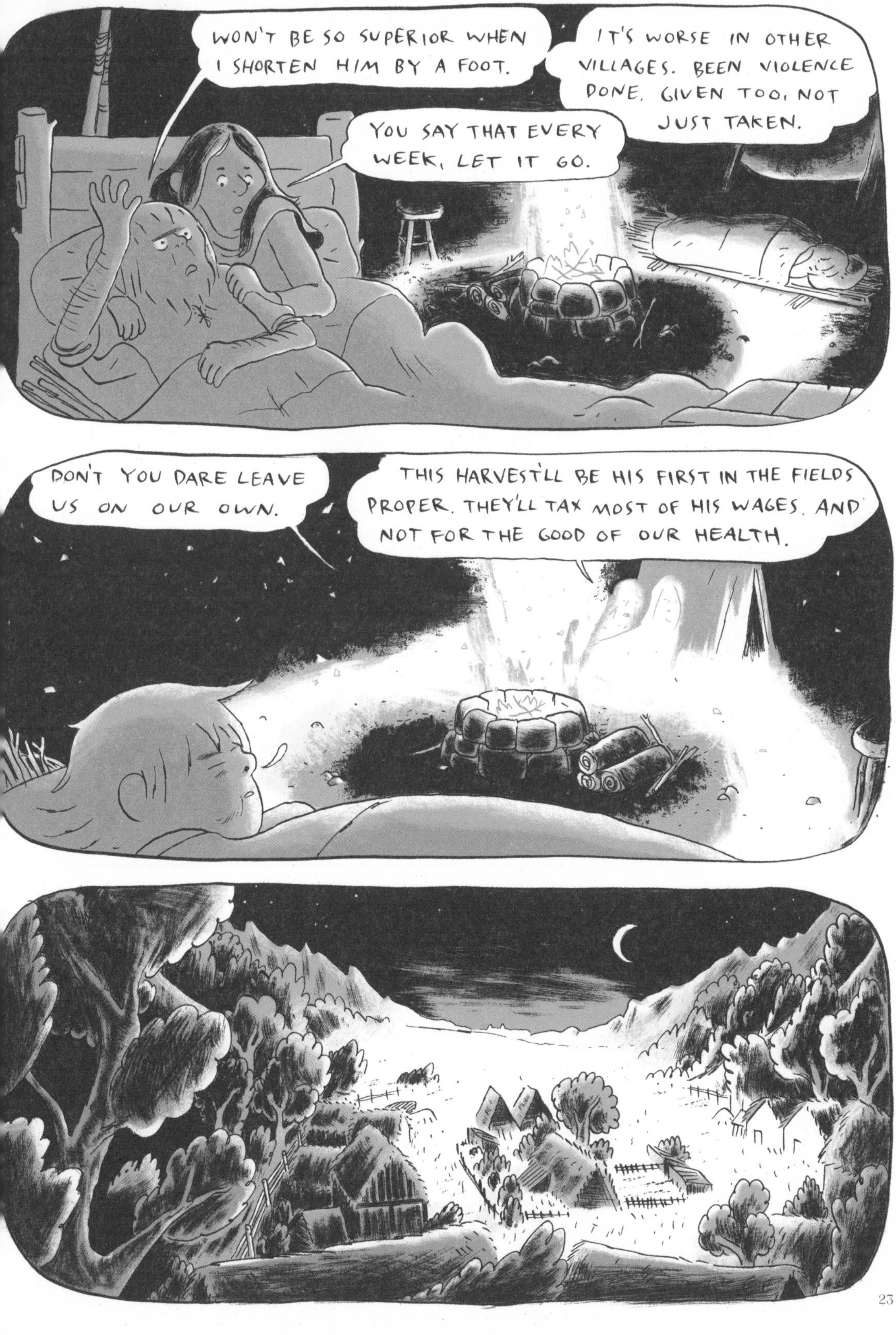
WON'T BE SO SUPERIOR WHEN I SHORTEN HIM BY A FOOT.
YOU SAY THAT EVERY WEEK, LET IT GO.
IT'S WORSE IN OTHER VILLAGES. BEEN VIOLENCE DONE. GIVEN TOO, NOT JUST TAKEN.
DON'T YOU DARE LEAVE US ON OUR OWN.
THIS HARVEST'LL BE HIS FIRST IN THE FIELDS PROPER. THEY'LL TAX MOST OF HIS WAGES. AND NOT FOR THE GOOD OF OUR HEALTH.

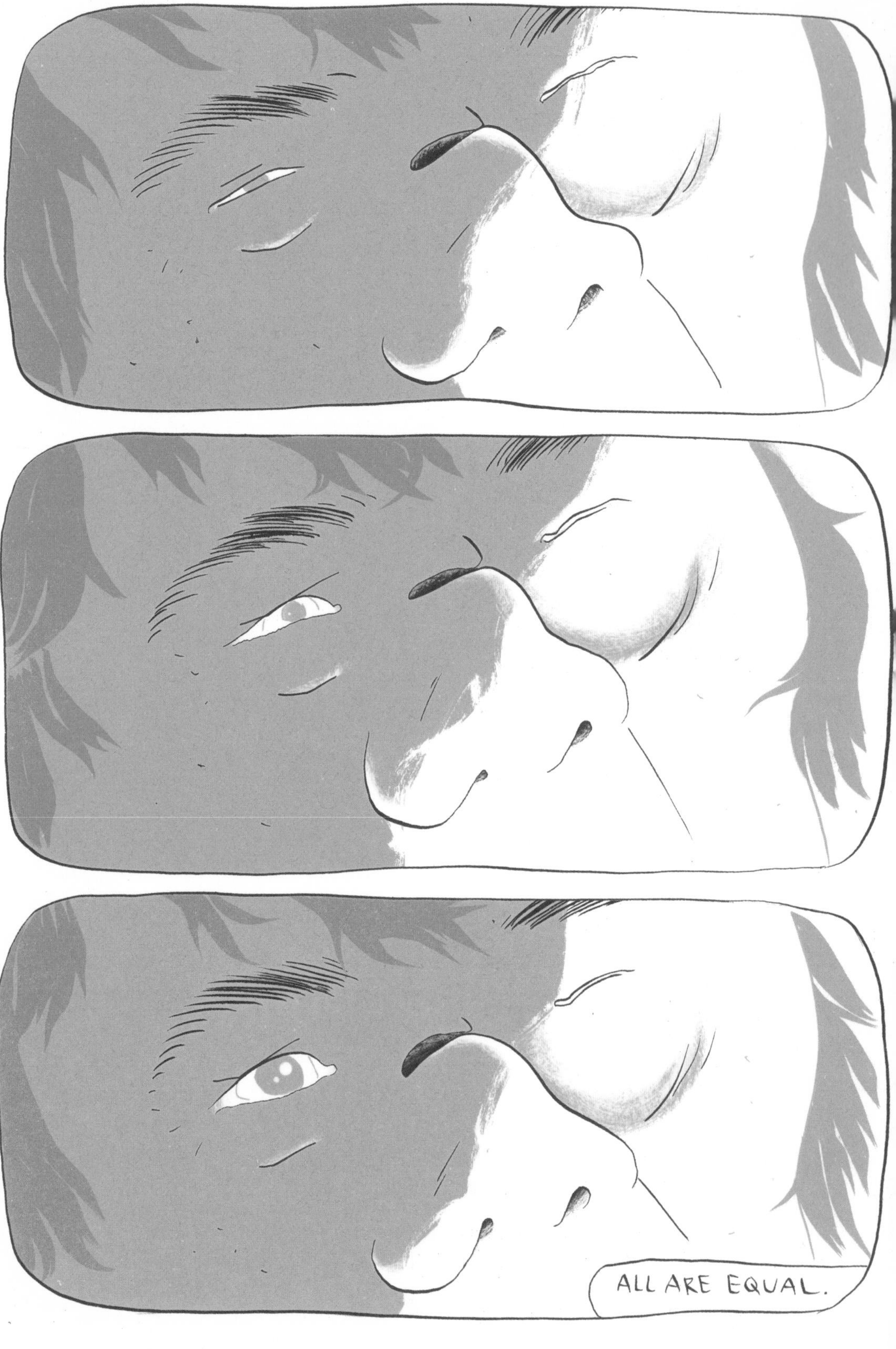
ALL ARE EQUAL.

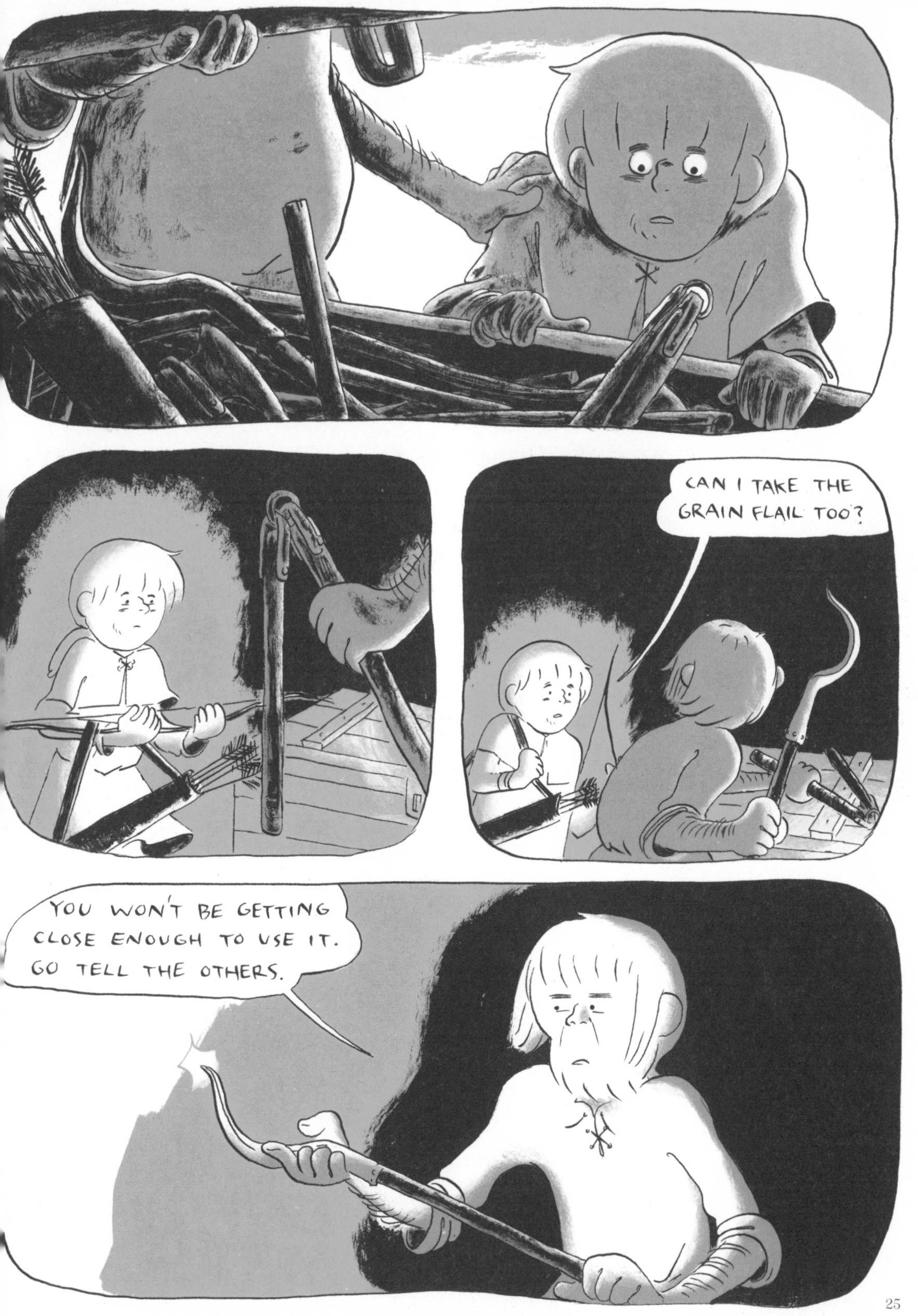
CAN I TAKE THE GRAIN FLAIL TOO?
YOU WON'T BE GETTING CLOSE ENOUGH TO USE IT. GO TELL THE OTHERS.

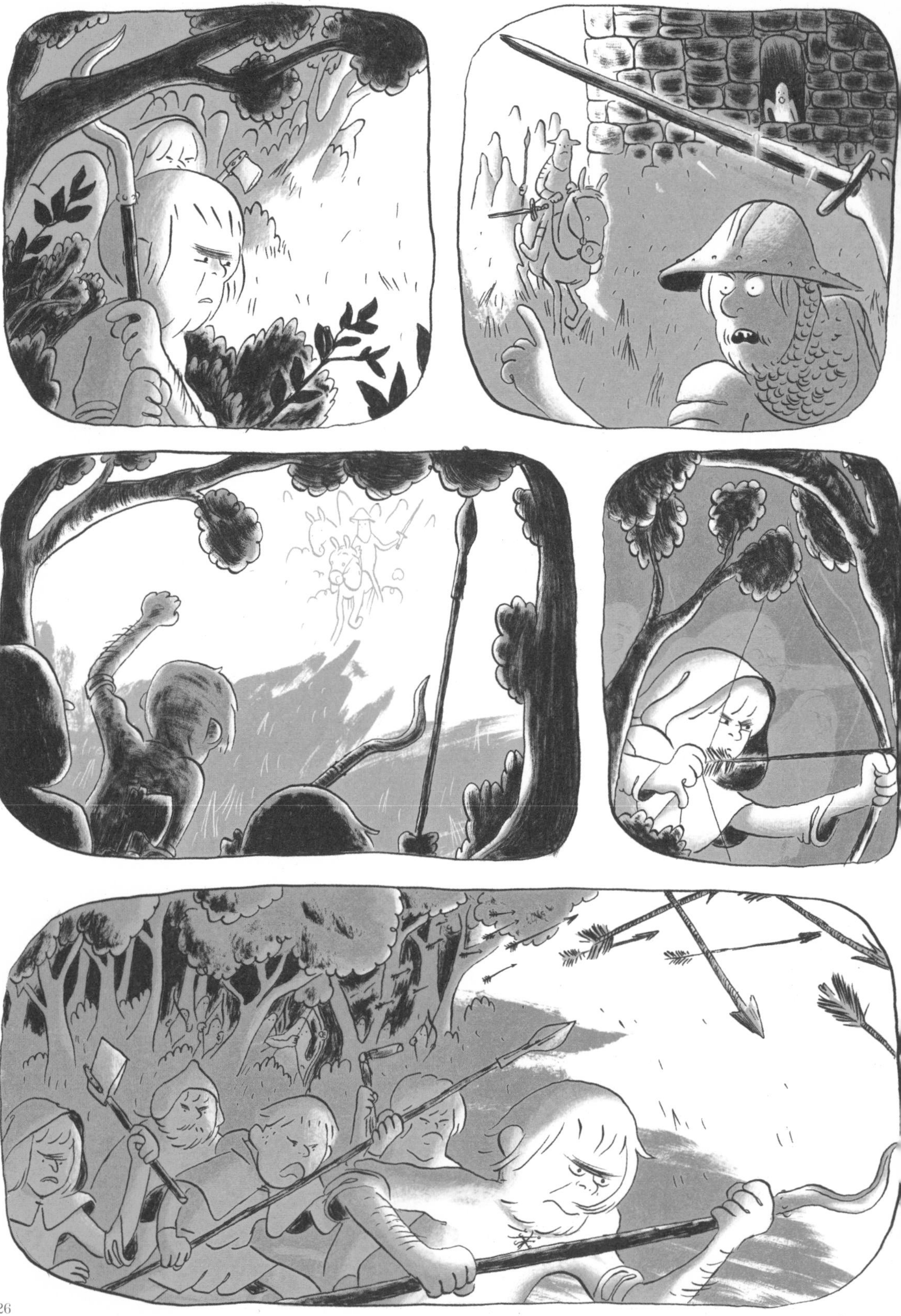

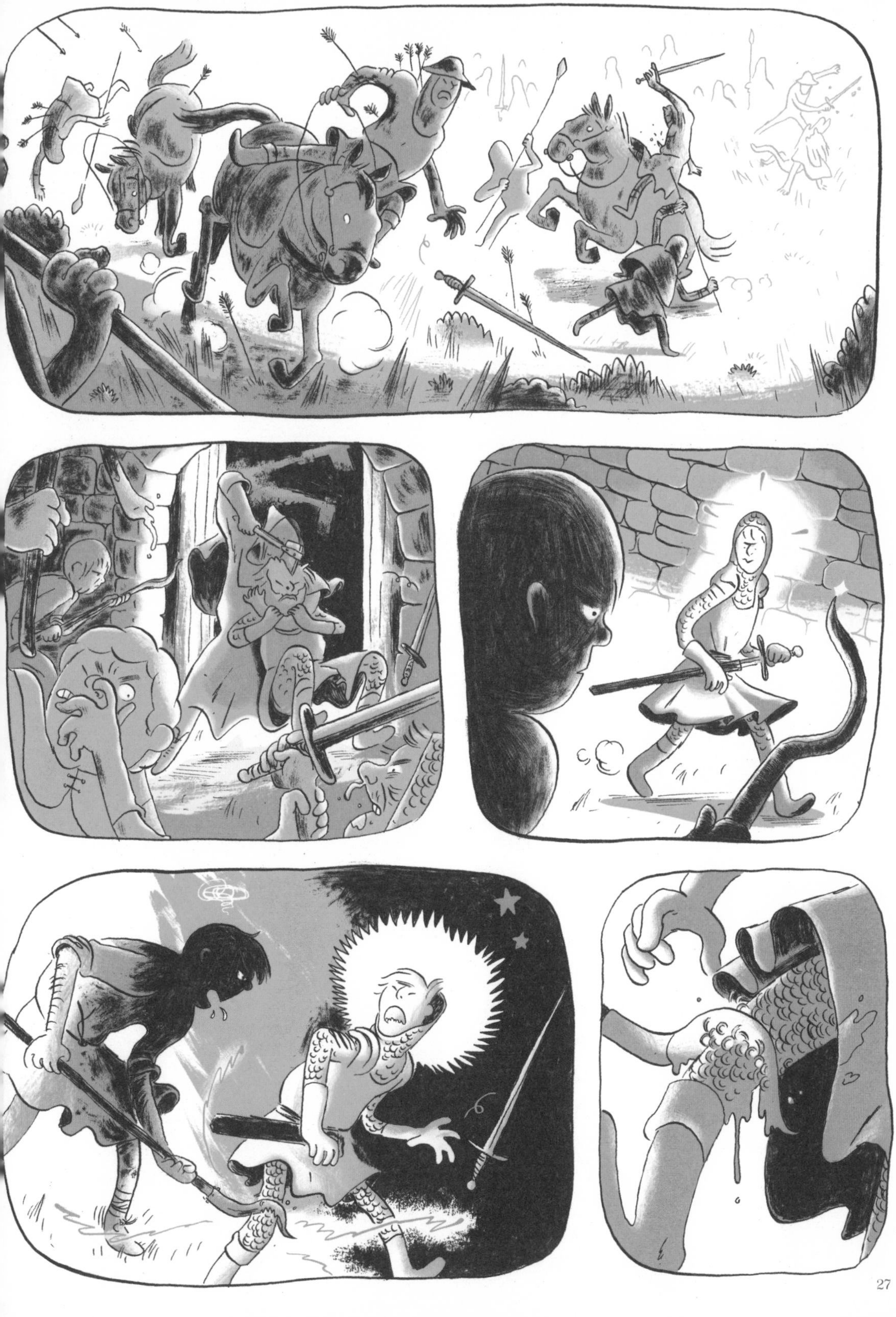

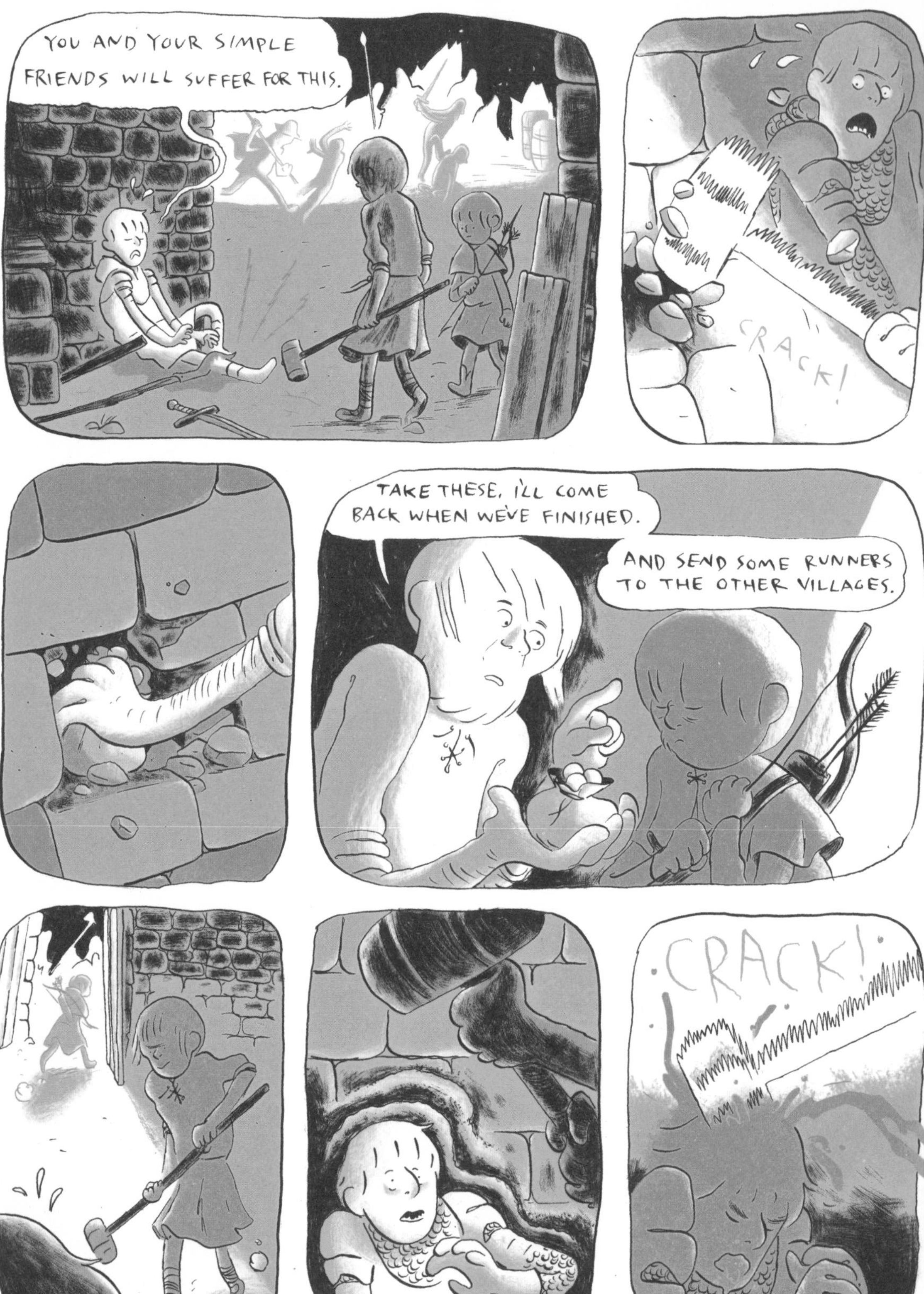

YOU AND YOUR SIMPLE FRIENDS WILL SUFFER FOR THIS.
CRACK!
TAKE THESE. I'LL COME BACK WHEN WE'VE FINISHED.
AND SEND SOME RUNNERS TO THE OTHER VILLAGES.
CRACK!

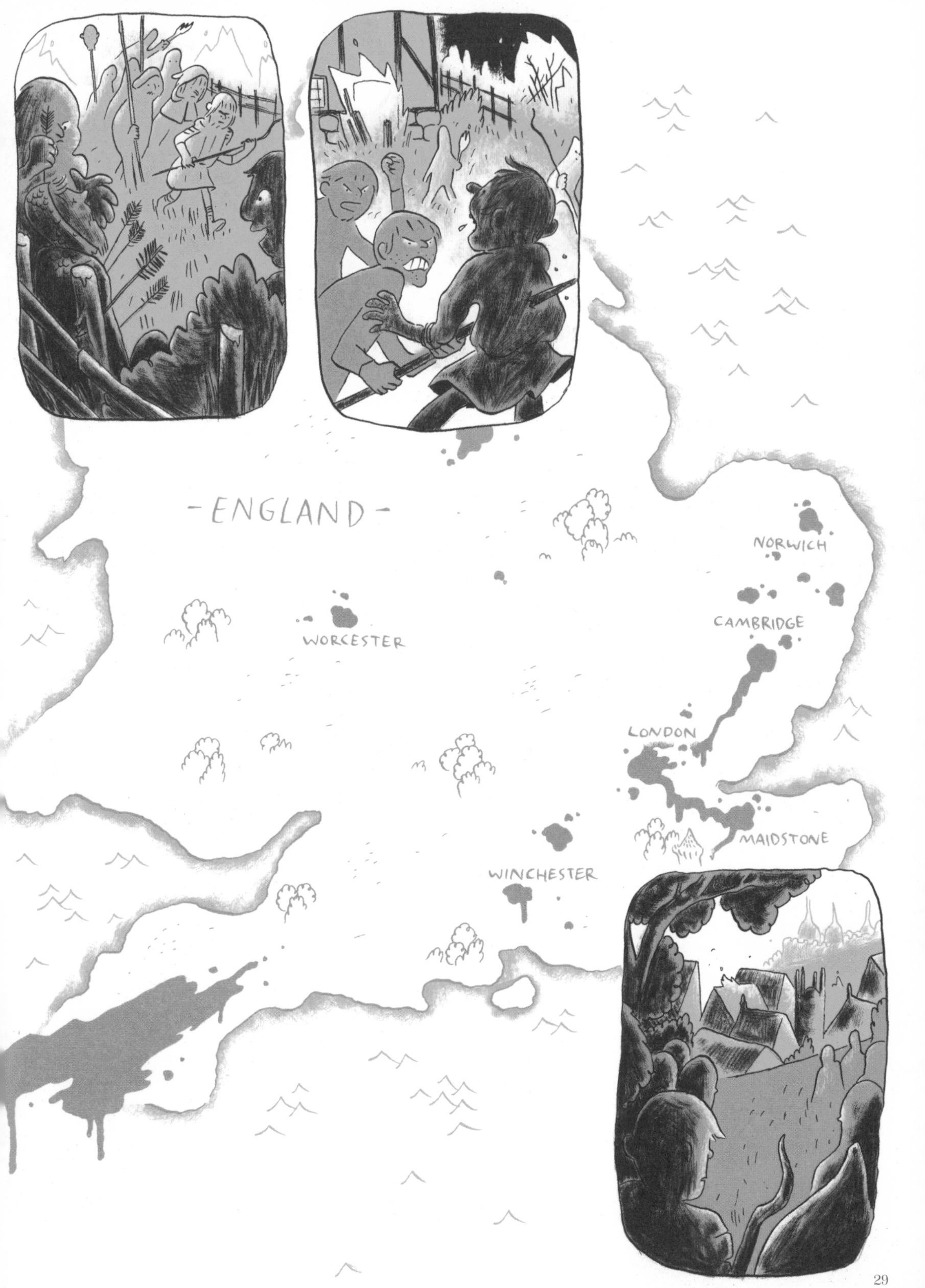
-ENGLAND-
NORWICH
WORCESTER
CAMBRIDGE
LONDON
MAIDSTONE
WINCHESTER

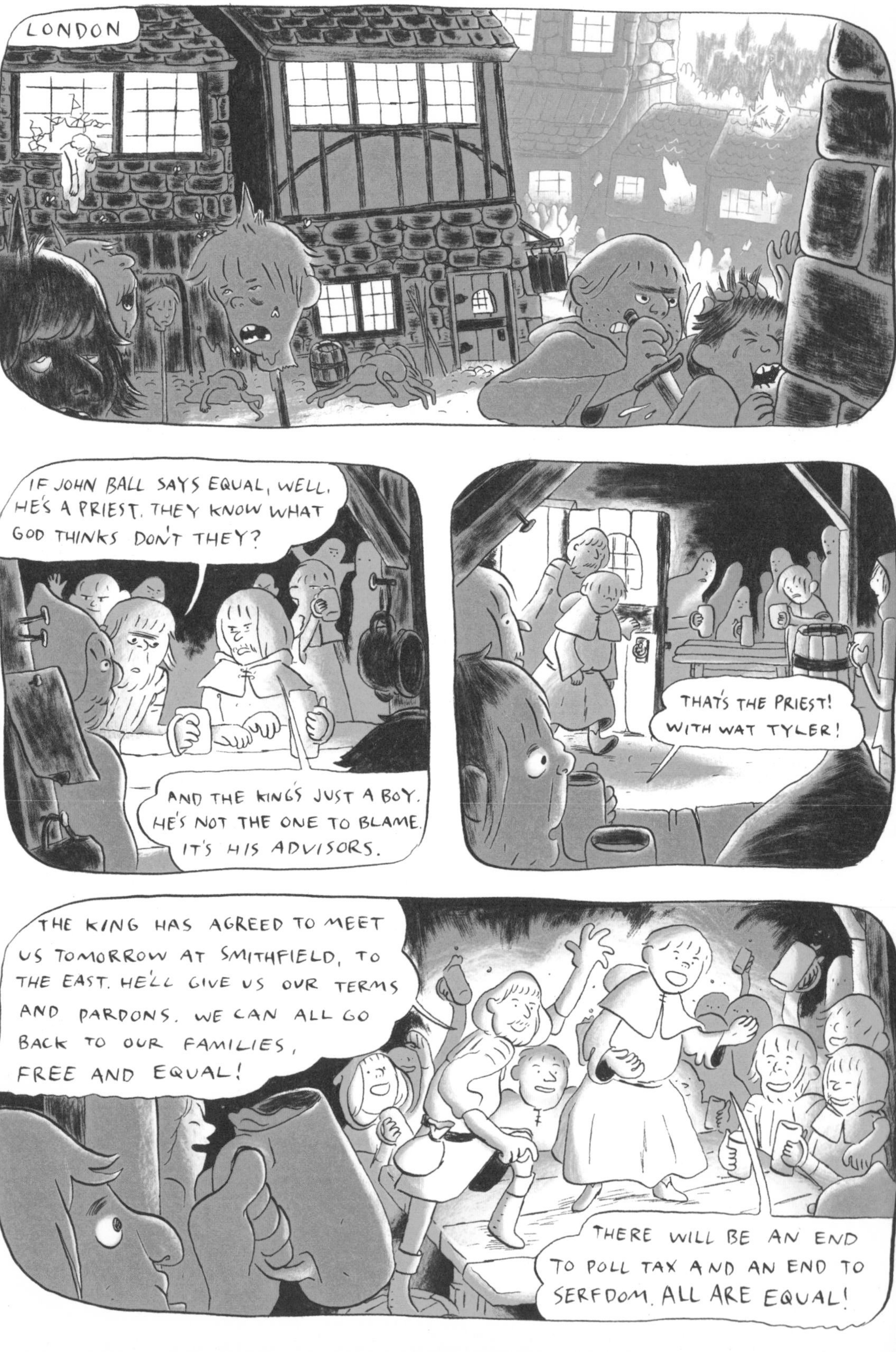
LONDON
IF JOHN BALL SAYS EQUAL, WELL. HE'S A PRIEST. THEY KNOW WHAT GOD THINKS DON'T THEY?
AND THE KING'S JUST A BOY. HE'S NOT THE ONE TO BLAME. IT'S HIS ADVISORS.
THAT'S THE PRIEST! WITH WAT TYLER!
THE KING HAS AGREED TO MEET US TOMORROW AT SMITHFIELD, TO THE EAST. HE'LL GIVE US OUR TERMS AND PARDONS. WE CAN ALL GO BACK TO OUR FAMILIES, FREE AND EQUAL!
THERE WILL BE AN END TO POLL TAX AND AN END TO SERFDOM. ALL ARE EQUAL!

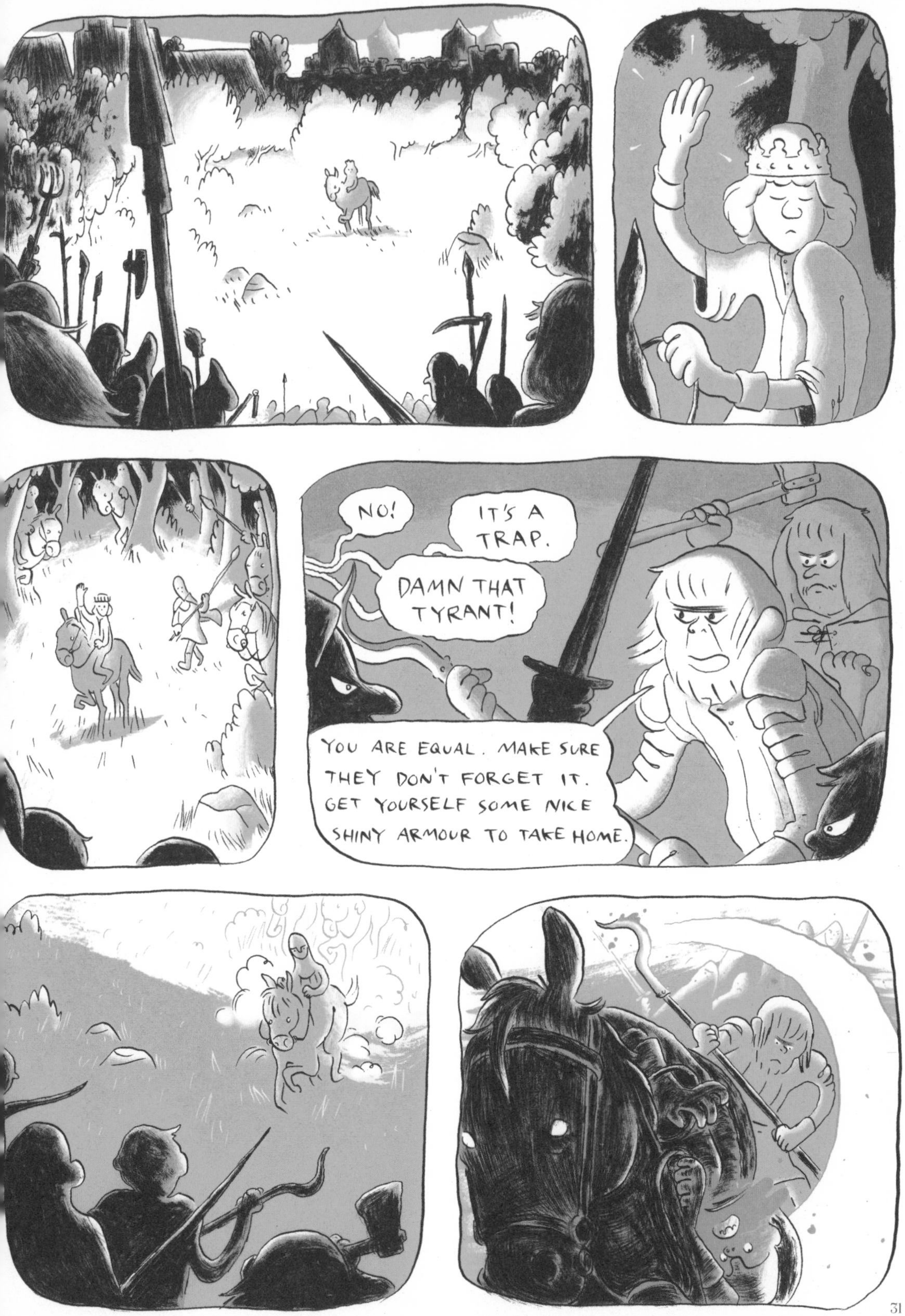
NO!
IT'S A TRAP.
DAMN THAT TYRANT!
YOU ARE EQUAL. MAKE SURE THEY DON'T FORGET IT. GET YOURSELF SOME NICE SHINY ARMOUR TO TAKE HOME.

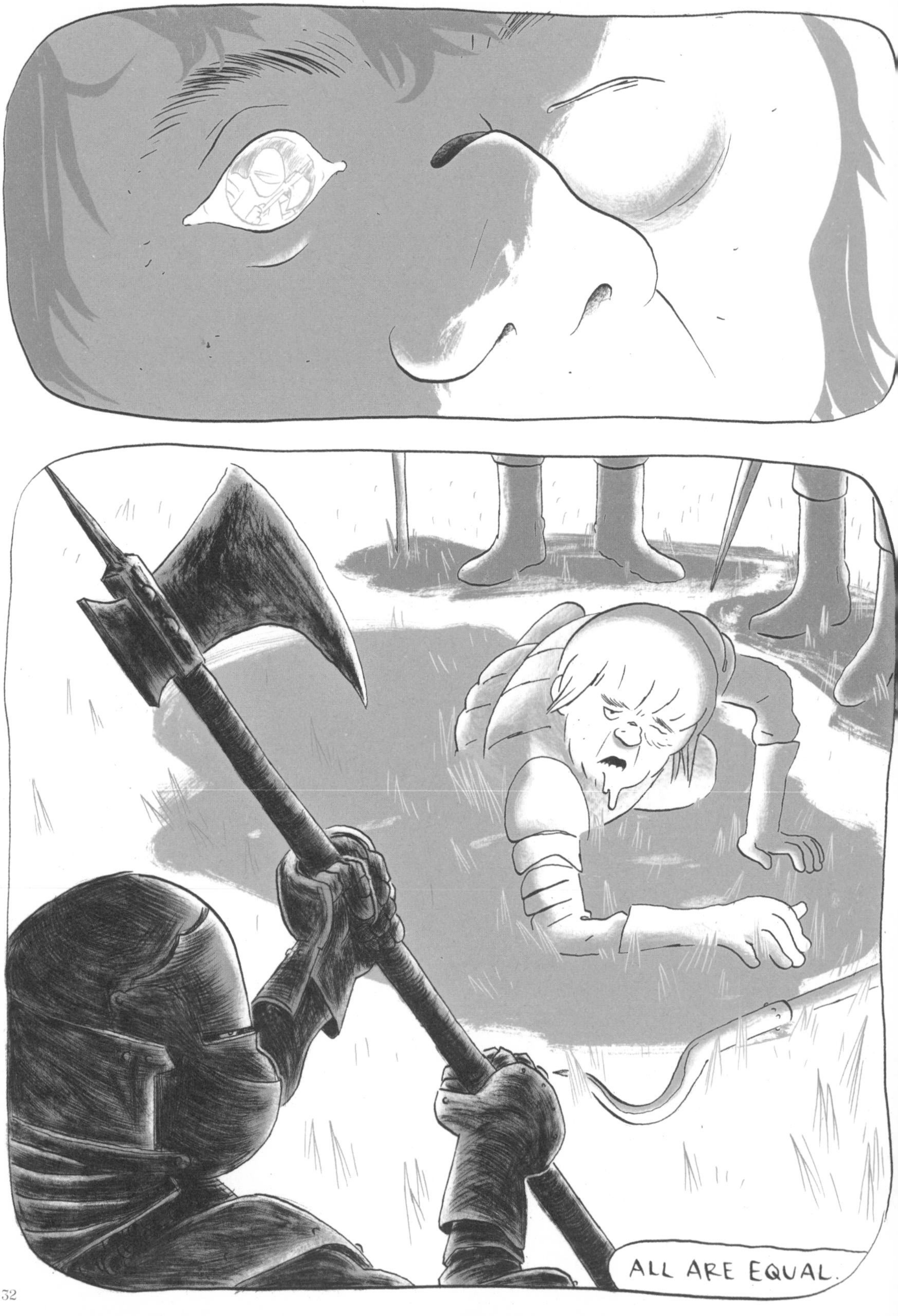
ALL ARE EQUAL.

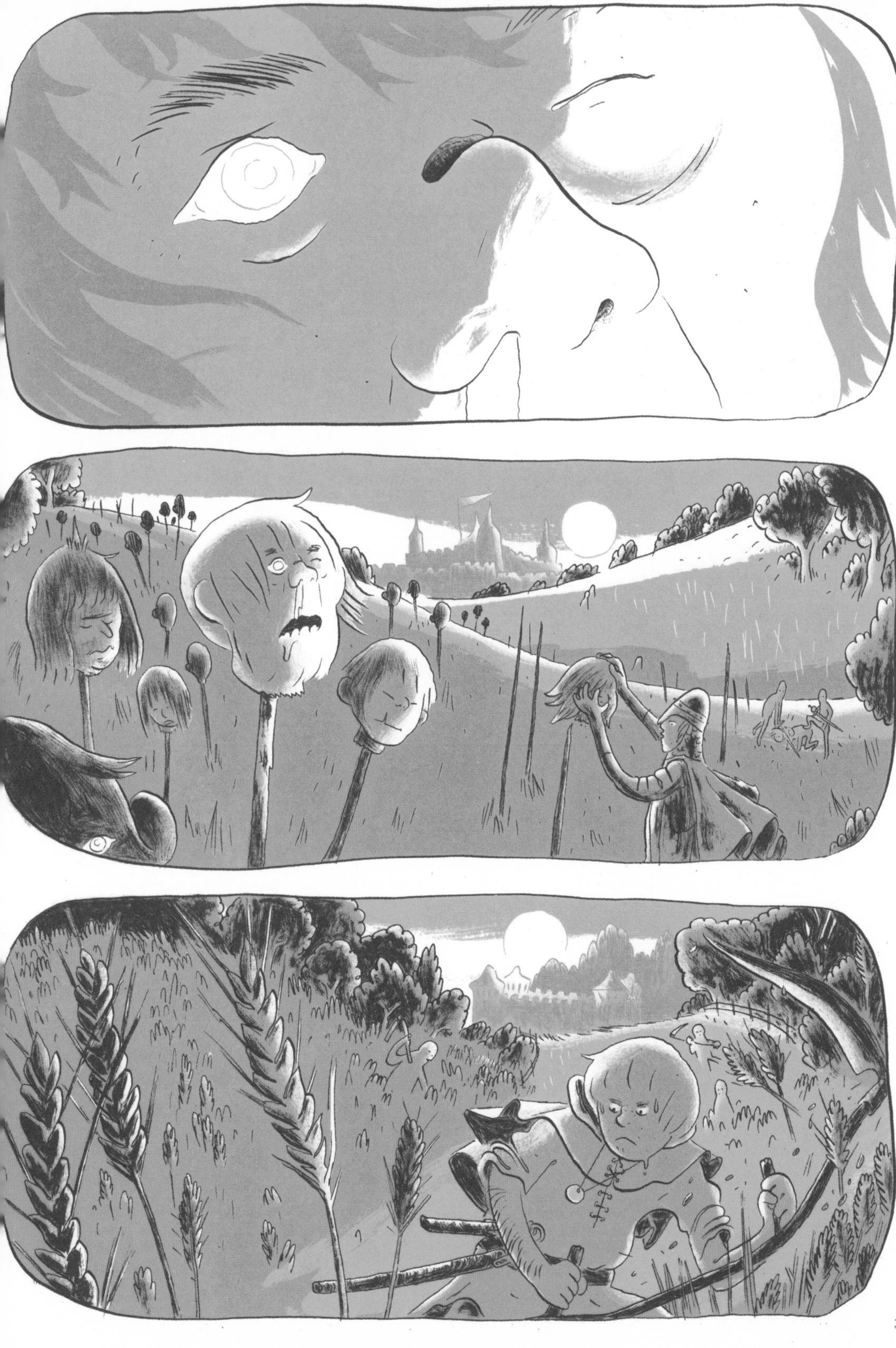

THE LABOURER
Historical Context

1. A fourteen year-old boy, King Richard II of the House Plantagenet, rules the Kingdom of England, and the 100 Years War with House Valois, rulers of the Kingdom of France, has been raging for decades. To pay for this costly war, the King's advisors have been imposing unsustainable taxes on an already impoverished population, including all children over fourteen years old, and granting Justices of the Peace extraordinary powers to enforce these taxes. The Kingdom is just beginning to recover from the Black Death plague epidemic that wiped out almost half of the population, not only in England but the whole of Europe. For the peasant classes, life is cheap, short, and unpleasant. It could be the backdrop to an epic fantasy story, but this is the reality of late medieval England.

2. Large portions of the population are "unfree" serfs, who labour on the land and cannot leave their villages to work elsewhere without permission from their landowner. However, after the Black Death manpower is in short supply and labourers can suddenly demand more for their work. This drives wages higher and consequently landowners' profits decrease, whilst the rural labourers' purchasing power increases. The authorities respond by introducing legislation to fix wages at pre-plague levels, make it illegal for the serfs to refuse work, and even prevent them from consuming expensive goods formerly only affordable to the gentry, with penalties for transgressors including branding and imprisonment. The royal government has never intervened like this before, nor allied itself with landowners in quite such a noticeable or unjust way.

3. Several incendiary events occur in quick succession, sparking riots across Kent and Essex. The accuracy of accounts of these events is unverifiable, but here are two rumours: firstly, in a village called Fobbing, the local Justice of the Peace tries to enforce a tax on the villagers twice despite their insistence that they have already paid. They beat him to death. Then in Maidstone, a Justice of the Peace attempts to look up a young girl's skirt to check if she is old enough to pay tax. The girl's father, Wat Tyler, kills the Justice. Wat Tyler is a former peasant soldier who uses his knowledge of warfare to unite his fellow villagers and rise up against the gentry. The revolt has begun.

4. News spreads of Wat Tyler and the riots happening throughout the region, and the number of peasants daring to revolt snowballs rapidly. Other influential peasants (likely ex soldiers from polearm units in the wars in France) lead their communities to join Wat Tyler and a radical priest, John Ball "the mad priest of Kent", who preaches equality for all and validates the rebel cause. The disparate groups of rioters unify into one peasant army, marching on London, ransacking every government building they come across, beheading thousands of wealthy people, and mounting heads on spikes.

5. At London they continue their bloodshed, marauding through the city setting fire to government buildings, burning tax records, and beheading prominent political and religious figures. They even break into the Tower of London – the only time it has ever been breached to this day – and remove the head of the Archbishop of Canterbury, Simon Sudbury, mounting it along with many others on a spike on London Bridge. Simon Sudbury's head can still be seen today, some 635 years later, although it is now kept at the church of St. Gregory at Sudbury in Suffolk.

6. The King meets with the peasant leaders at Mile End in London, and agrees to all of their demands, including ending serfdom. Satisfied, many of the rebels leave London and journey home. The next day, the King meets the peasants again in Smithfield just outside London to discuss the terms of their demands. However, this time an army of well-armed knights join him, and after discussions turn sour – it is not clear precisely why – the peasants and their leaders are slaughtered. Their heads are similarly mounted on spikes as a warning to any future rebellions.

7. The revolt was effectively over by the end of summer. The King did not keep his promises and little changed for the peasants. However, there never was another poll tax and peasants were treated with more respect through fear of further uprisings. The Peasant's Revolt of 1381 was a key turning point in attitudes towards the common man, and sowed the seed from which the Human Rights law we know today would eventually grow.

Factual Background
at Scotney Castle

1. The original Scotney Castle was built around 1378-1380, by Roger de Ashburnham. At this time it was illegal for landowners to build crenallations and other fortifications on their property as this would give them a base from which to attack the king. However, the threat of invasion from France was perceived to be so severe that in parts of England these laws were relaxed. Landowners used this opportunity to fortify their manor houses in what seems to be a show of wealth rather than increased security. It is likely that Scotney Castle would originally have looked something like nearby Bodiam Castle, a majestic castle built around the same time; impressive to behold but would have been unlikely to withstand a sustained attack.

2. In the book, "Provincial Life: The Knightly Families of Kent and Sussex", there is an account of a riot that took place two years after the castle was built. This falls very neatly into the time that peasants across the region were rising up and rioting. In researching the story at Scotney Castle, it seems quite likely to me that the Peasant's Revolt of 1381 could have played a role in this castle's history.

Darell Family Tree
2nd family to take the castle

—

From the Lancaster Period to the Tudor Period

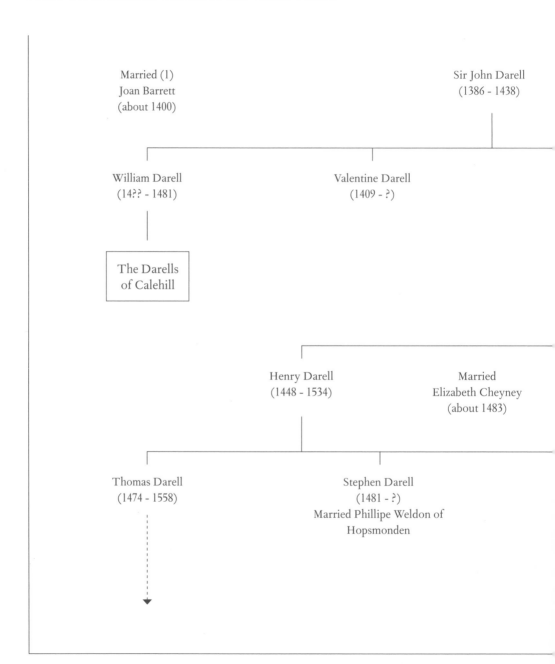

Married (1)
Joan Barrett
(about 1400)

Sir John Darell
(1386 - 1438)

William Darell
(14?? - 1481)

Valentine Darell
(1409 - ?)

The Darells
of Calehill

Henry Darell
(1448 - 1534)

Married
Elizabeth Cheyney
(about 1483)

Thomas Darell
(1474 - 1558)

Stephen Darell
(1481 - ?)
Married Phillipe Weldon of
Hopsmonden

NOTE:

This information has been derived from various early
documents and we cannot be sure of the accuracy

Married (2)
Florence Chichele
(in 1418)

John Darell
(1420 - before 1438)

Robert Darell
(1426 - ?)

Thomas Darell
(1422 - 1470)

Married
Thomasine Gresley
(about 1460)

Agnes Darell
(1450 - ?)

Florence Darell
(1456 - ?)

Richard Darell
(1495 - 1568)

The Darells
of Calehill

This branch of the family tree continues on page 62

Darell Family Tree

The Elizabethan Period, the Stuart Era, Civil War and the Commonwealth

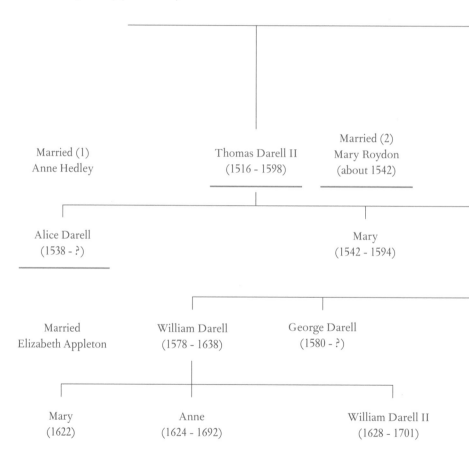

Married (1)
Elizabeth Horne
(in 1513) (11 children)

Married (1)
Anne Hedley

Thomas Darell II
(1516 - 1598)

Married (2)
Mary Roydon
(about 1542)

Alice Darell
(1538 - ?)

Mary
(1542 - 1594)

Married
Elizabeth Appleton

William Darell
(1578 - 1638)

George Darell
(1580 - ?)

Mary
(1622)

Anne
(1624 - 1692)

William Darell II
(1628 - 1701)

NOTE:

This information has been derived from various early documents and we cannot be sure of the accuracy

Thomas Darell
(1474 - 1558)

Married (2)
Alice Whetenhall
(in 1537)

Frances
(1540 - 1574)

Henry Darell
(1543 - 1630)

Married
Margeret Gage of Fide Place
(in 1580)

Frances (1546 - ?)
Phillip (1548 - ?)
Margaret (1550 - ?)
Helen (1553 - ?)

Thomas Darell (1582 - ?)
Henry Darell (1584 - ?)
John Darell (1586 - ?)

—— Persons marked red feature in the story 'The Priest'

THE PRIEST
by Briony May Smith

The monarchy is in radical transition, and the religion
of the country with it; Church of England under Henry
VIII, briefly Protestant under Edward VI, Catholic under
Mary I, and Protestant again under Elizabeth I. All in the
space of just 11 years. It is a time of immense fear, full
of plots, intrigues and conspiracies involving the highest
levels of society. Brutal executions are commonplace
and nobody is exempt. The family at Scotney Castle live
under a cloud of suspicion due to their extreme religious
views, and refusal to partake in the practices of a country
whose religious demands are suddenly at odds with their
own. As always in religious power struggles, it is the
moderates who suffer…

Elizabethan Era
The English Reformation
- c.1590 -

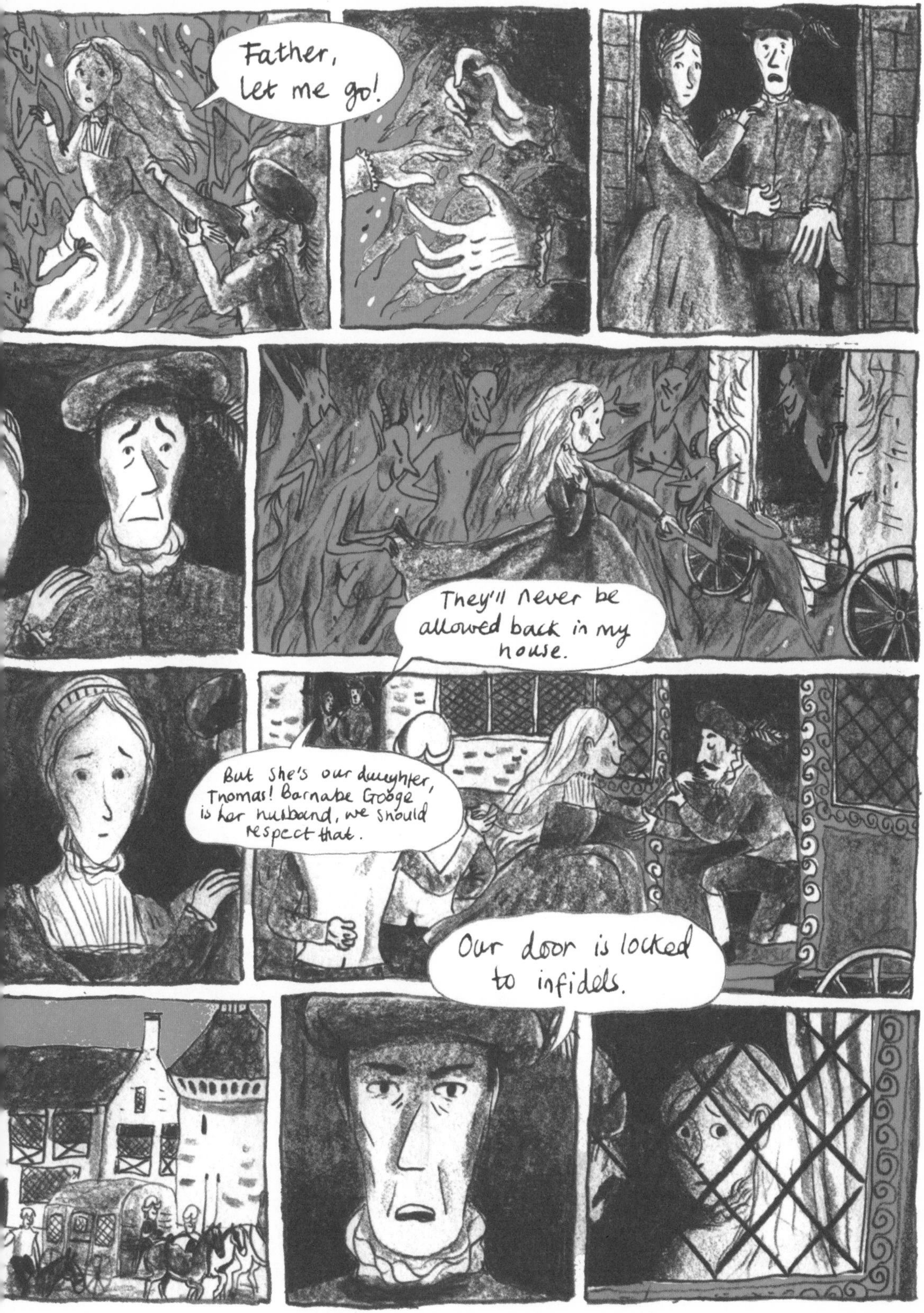
Father, let me go!
They'll never be allowed back in my house.
But she's our daughter, Thomas! Barnabe Googe is her husband, we should respect that.
Our door is locked to infidels.

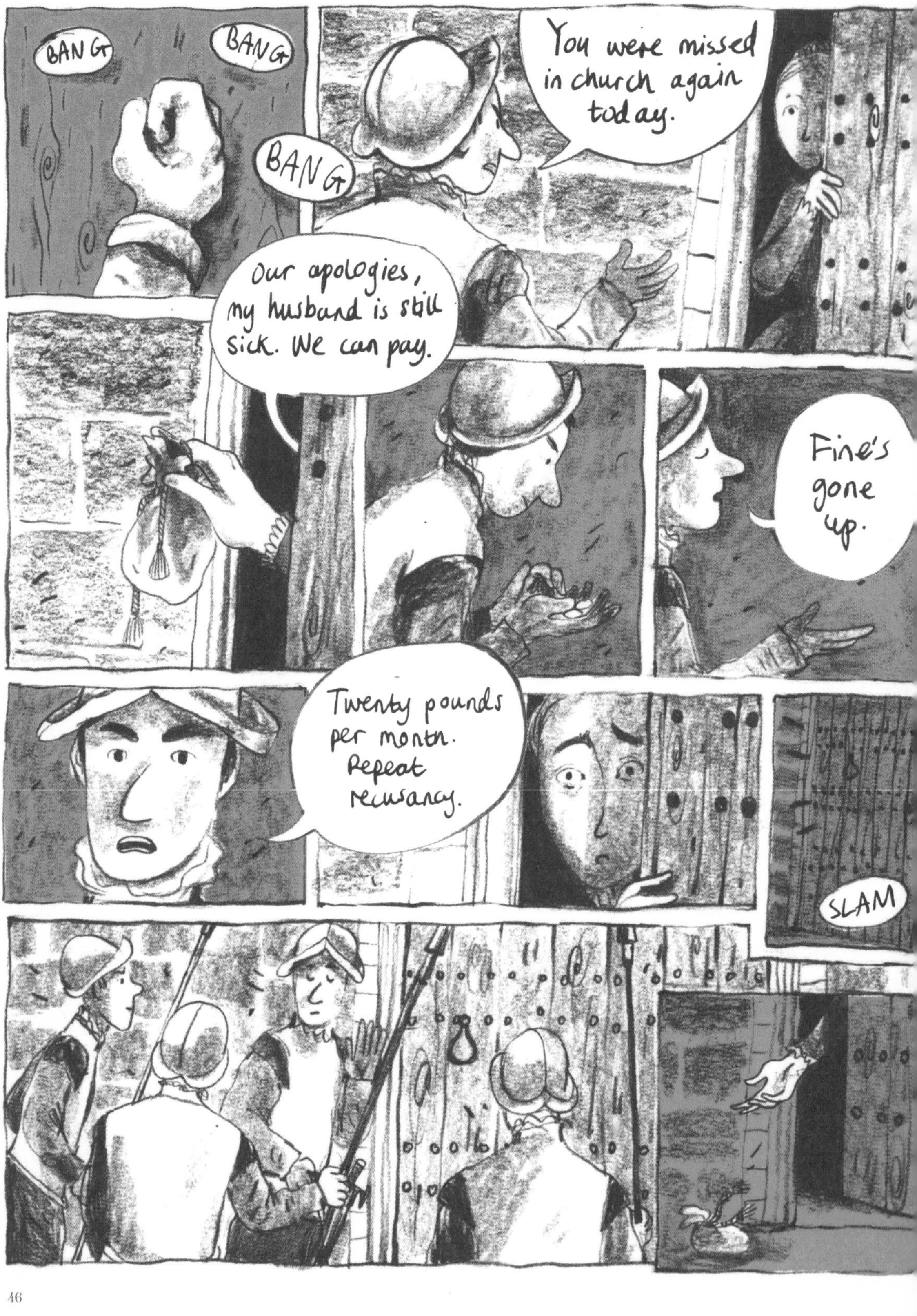
BANG
BANG
BANG
You were missed in church again today.
Our apologies, my husband is still sick. We can pay.
Fine's gone up.
Twenty pounds per month. Repeat recusancy.
SLAM

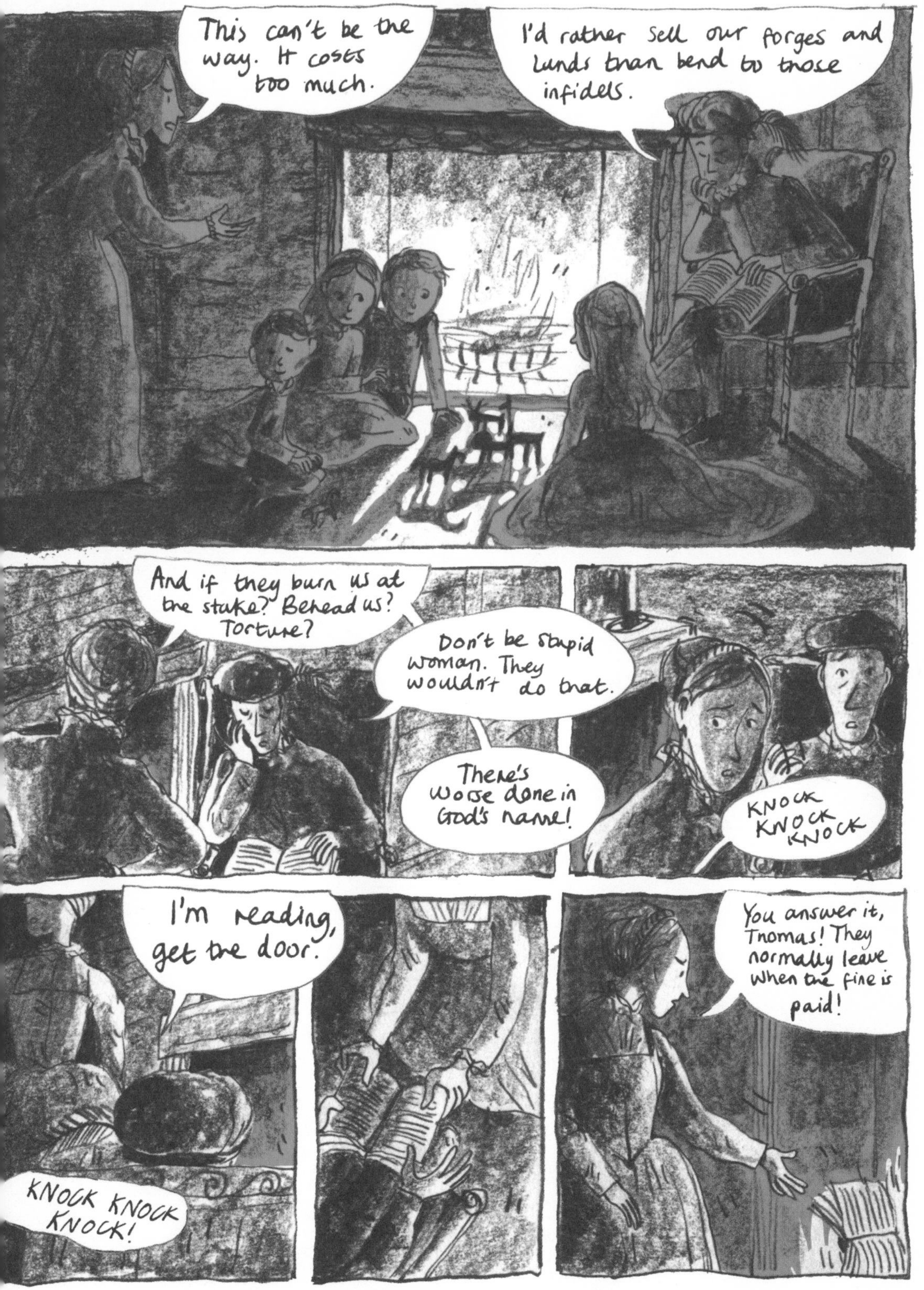
This can't be the way. It costs too much.
I'd rather sell our forges and lands than bend to those infidels.
And if they burn us at the stake? Behead us? Torture?
Don't be stupid woman. They wouldn't do that.
There's worse done in God's name!
KNOCK KNOCK KNOCK
I'm reading, get the door.
KNOCK KNOCK KNOCK!
You answer it, Thomas! They normally leave when the fine is paid!

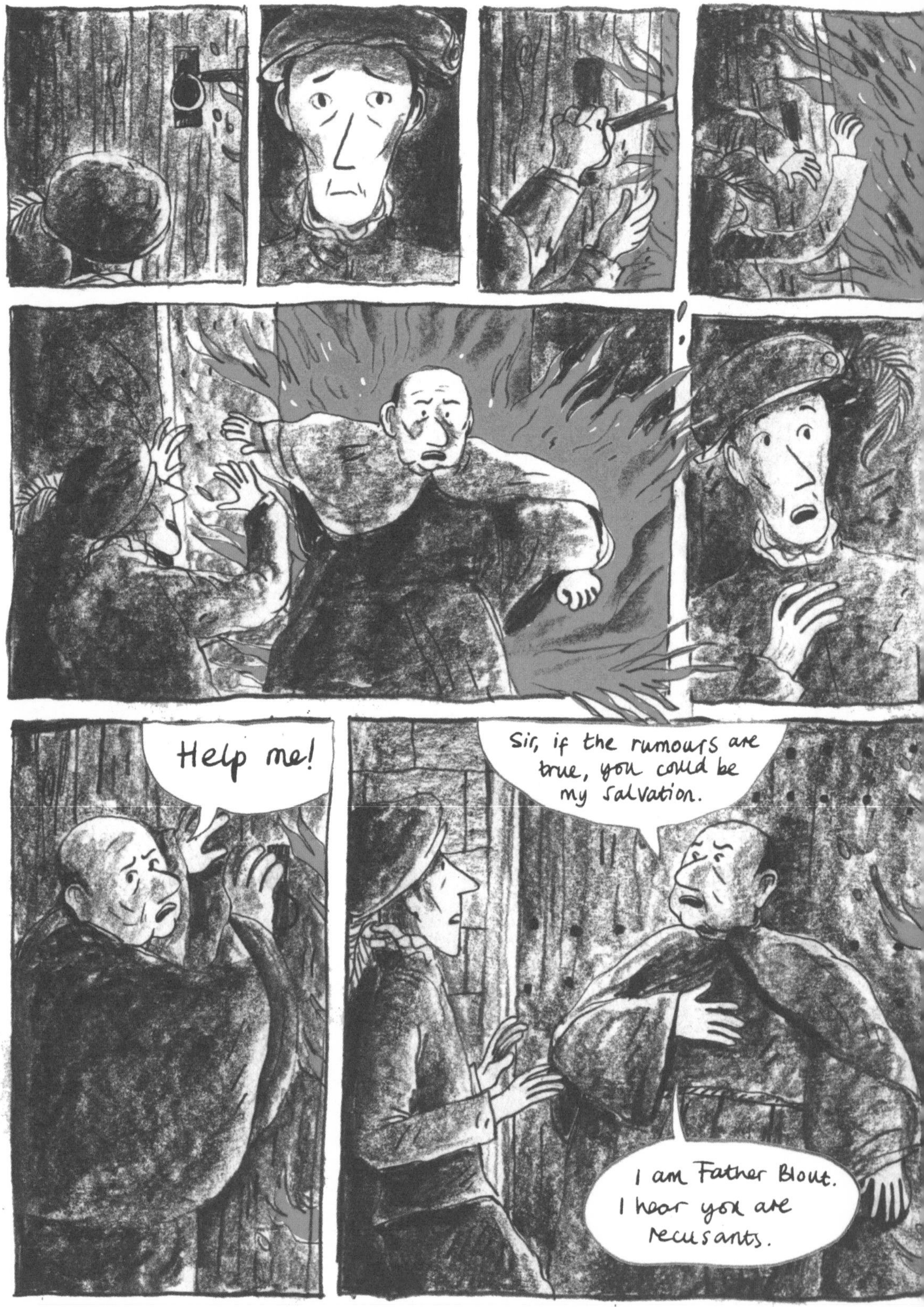
Help me!
Sir, if the rumours are true, you could be my salvation.
I am Father Blout. I hear you are recusants.

What if it's a trick? To expose us. Damn us to the gibbet.

Madam, I'm in mortal danger! I swam the moat to escape pursuit. If you have faith, you must help.

Apologies Father. You risk much in coming here. These days are filled with fear.

Perhaps you could lead us in Holy Mass? Hear our confessions.

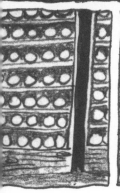

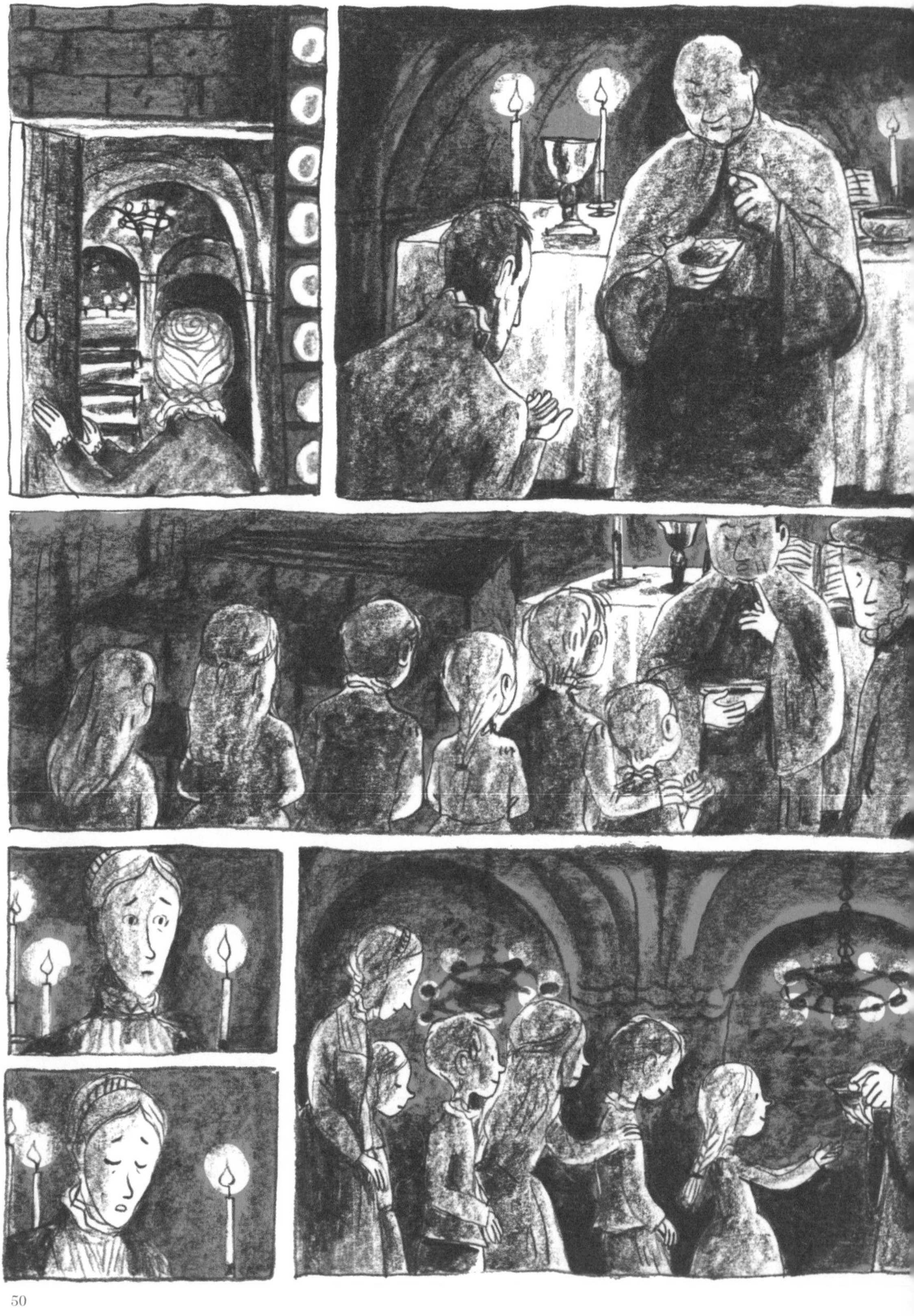

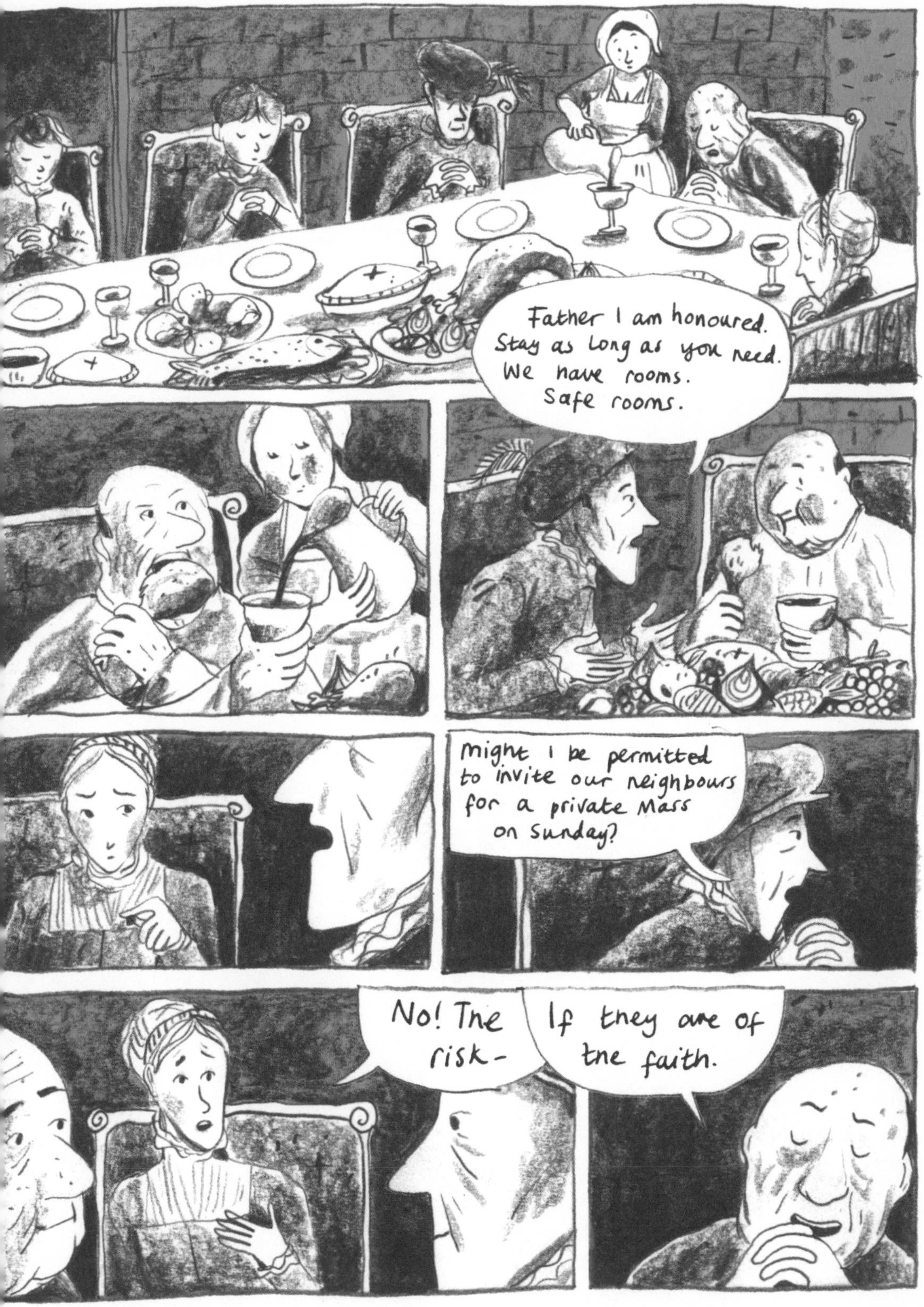
Father I am honoured. Stay as long as you need. We have rooms. Safe rooms.
might I be permitted to invite our neighbours for a private Mass on Sunday?
No! The risk-
If they are of the faith.

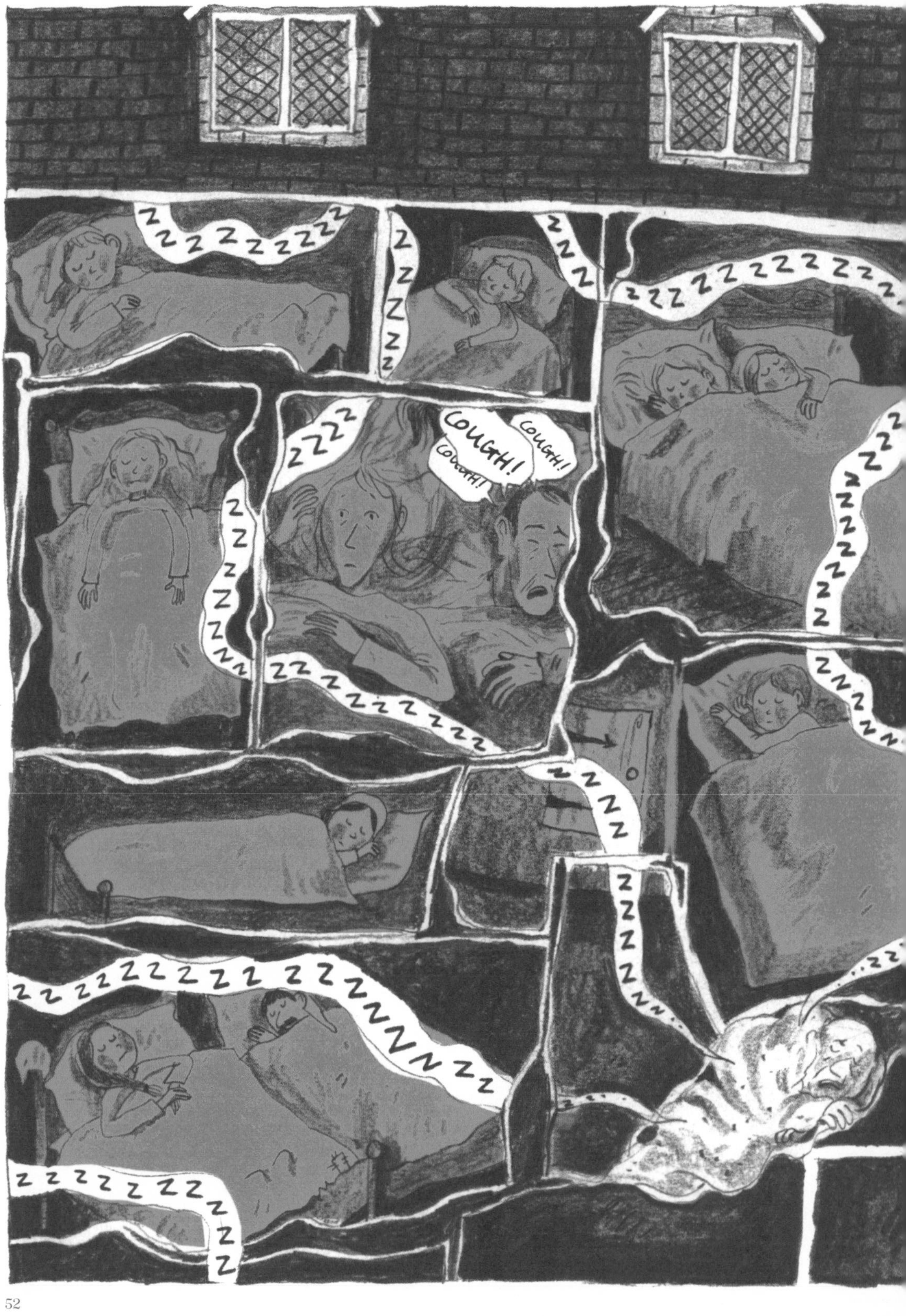
COUGH!
COUGH!
COUGH!

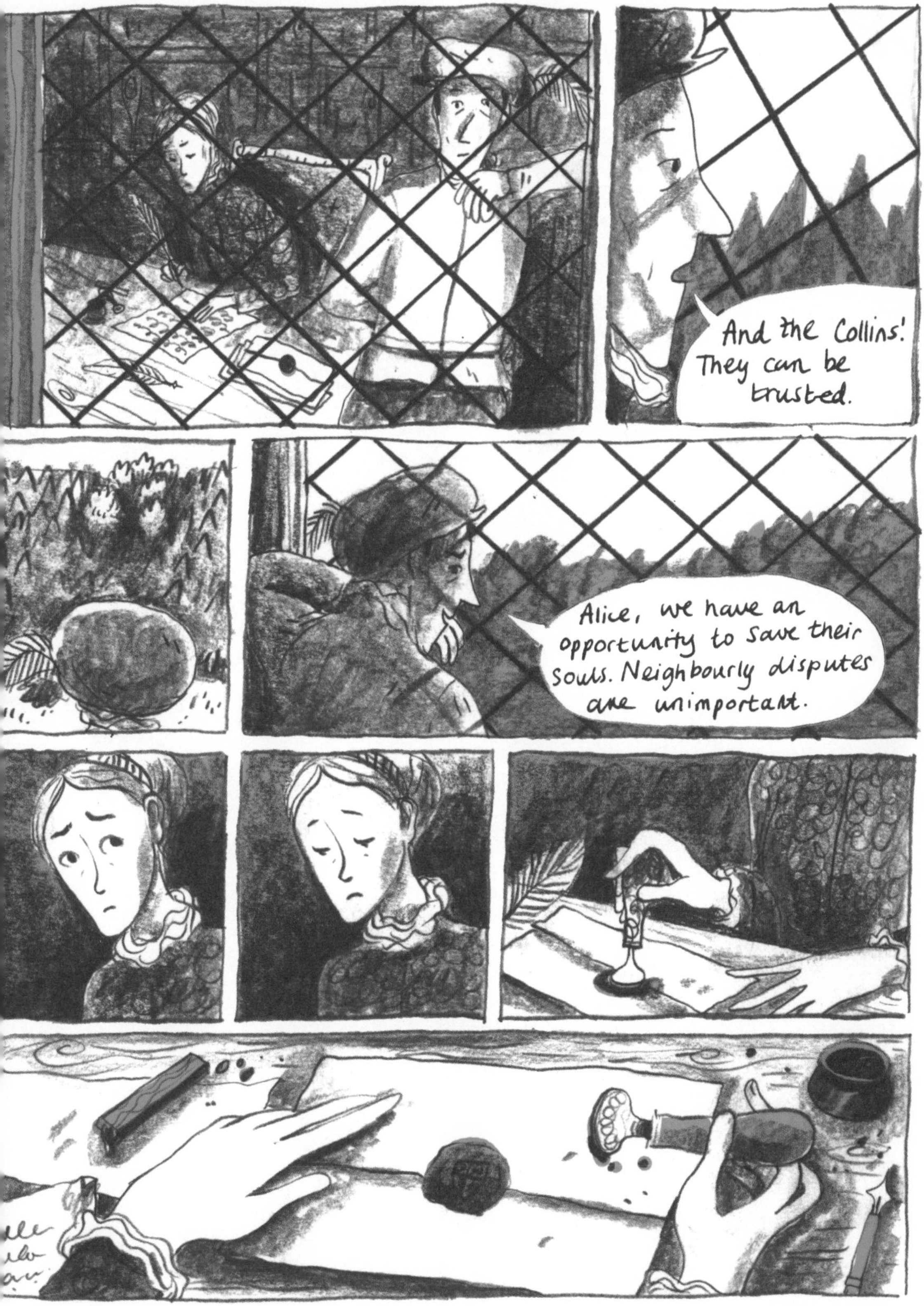
And the Collins! They can be trusted.
Alice, we have an opportunity to save their souls. Neighbourly disputes are unimportant.

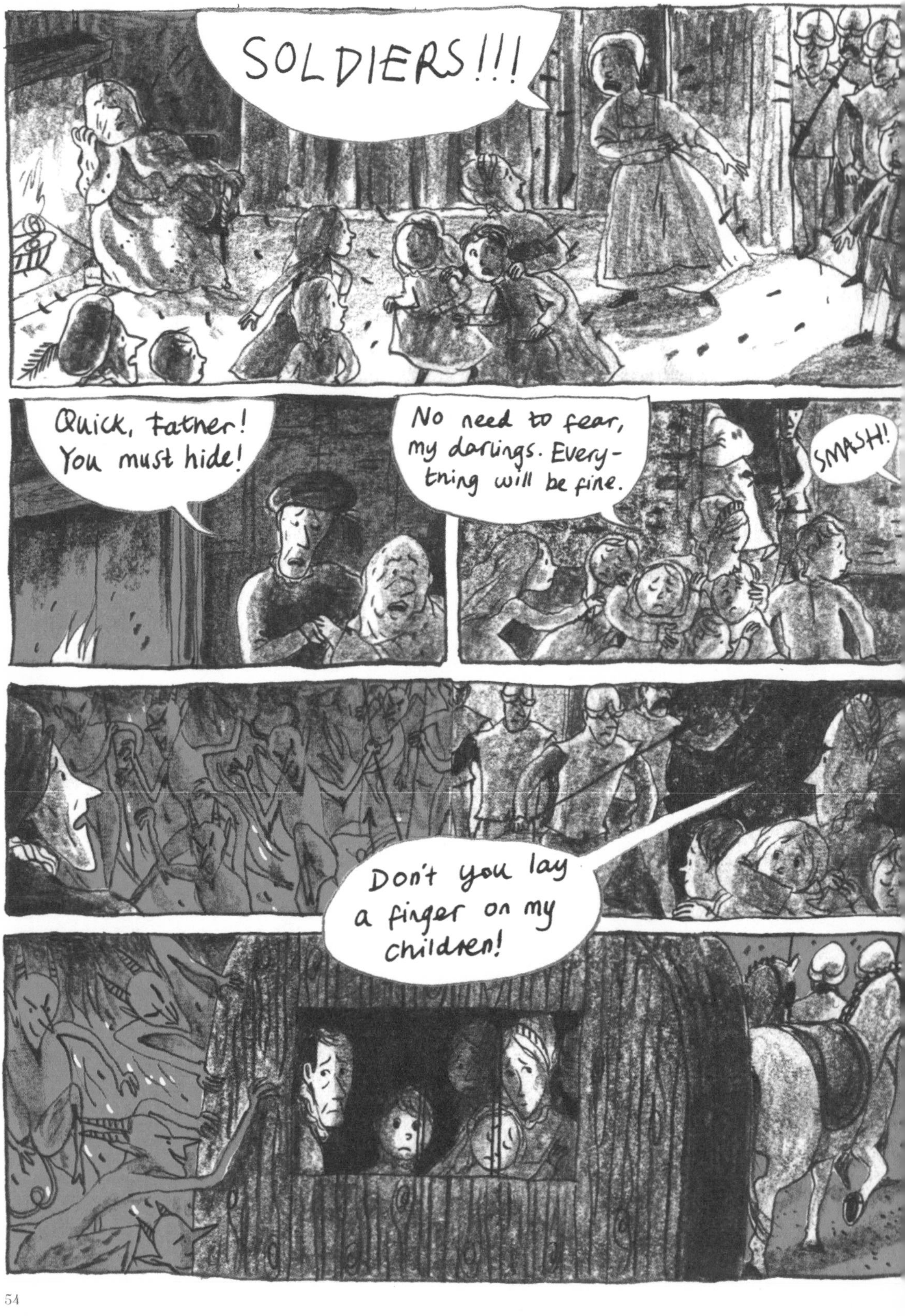
SOLDIERS!!!
Quick, father! You must hide!
No need to fear, my darlings. Every-thing will be fine.
SMASH!
Don't you lay a finger on my children!

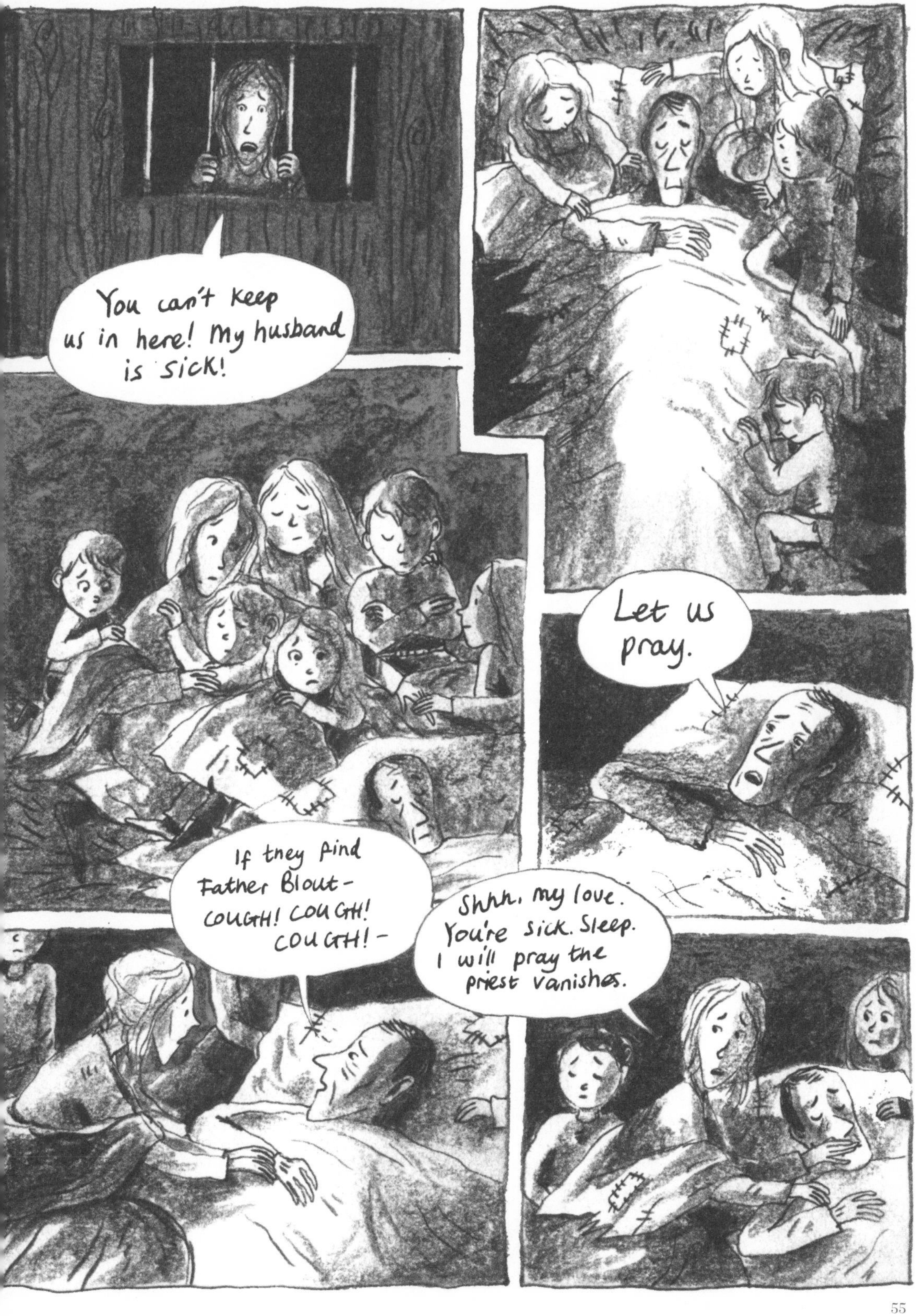
You can't keep us in here! My husband is sick!
Let us pray.
If they find Father Blout - COUGH! COUGH! COUGH! -
Shhh, my love. You're sick. Sleep. I will pray the priest vanishes.

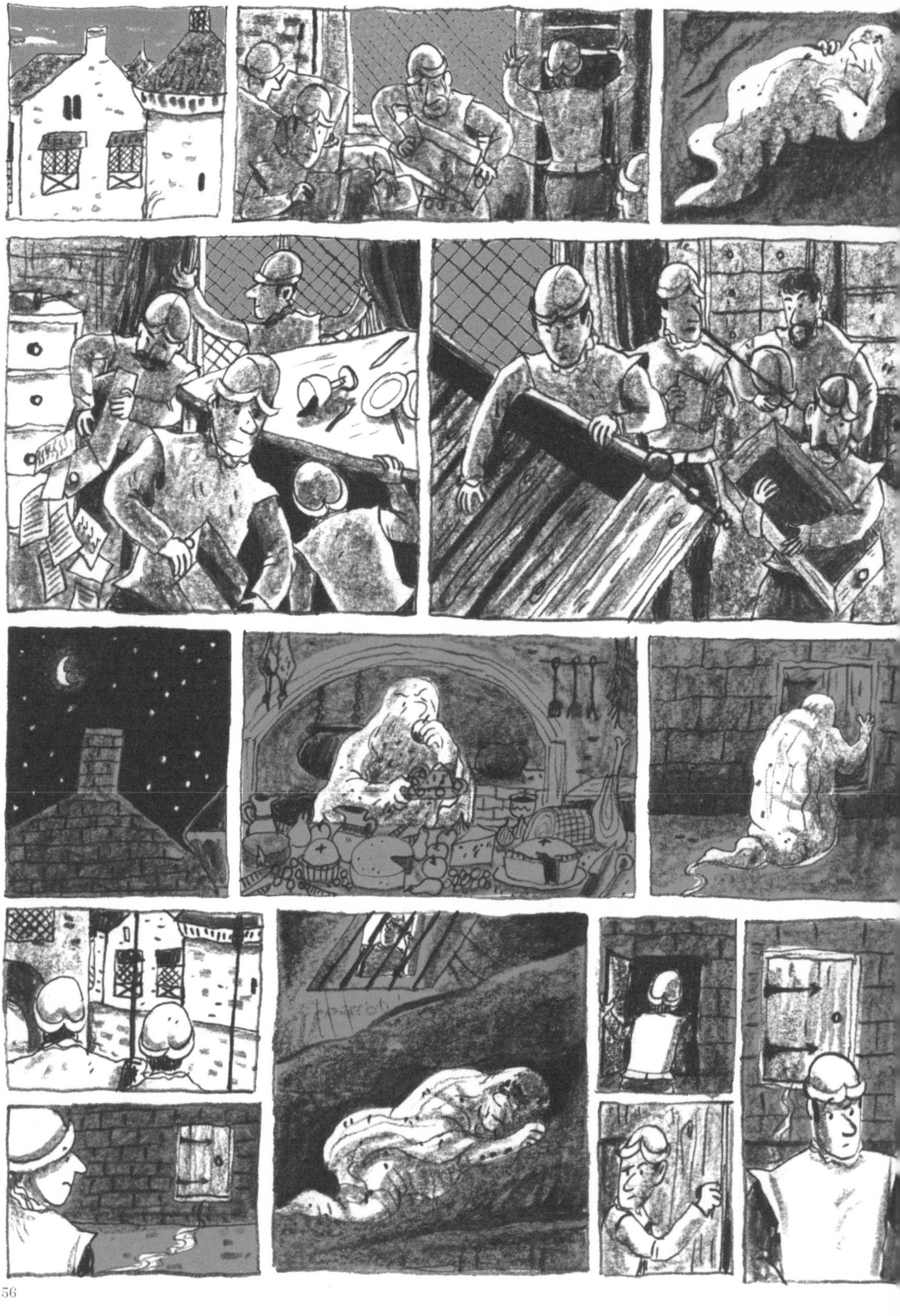

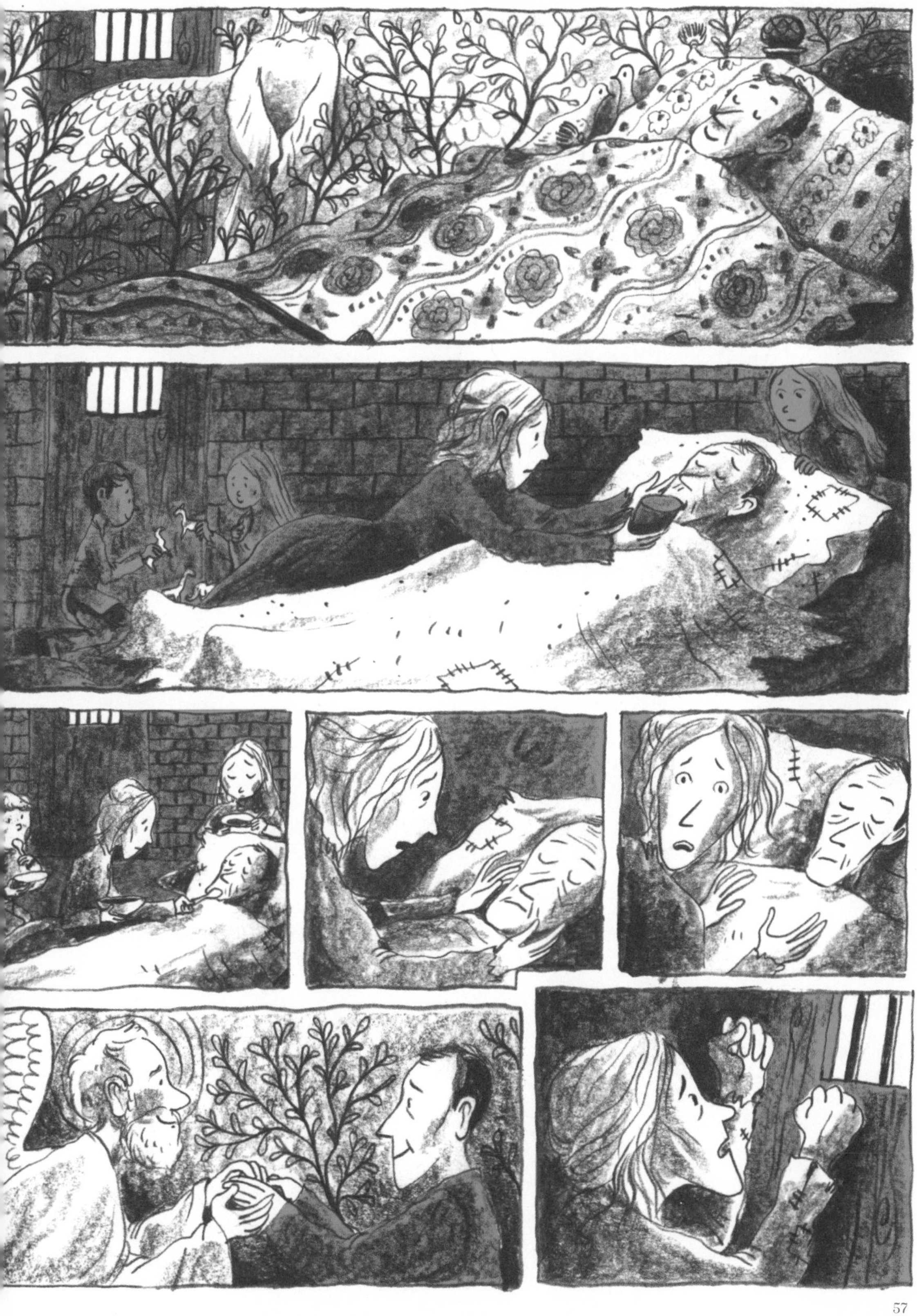

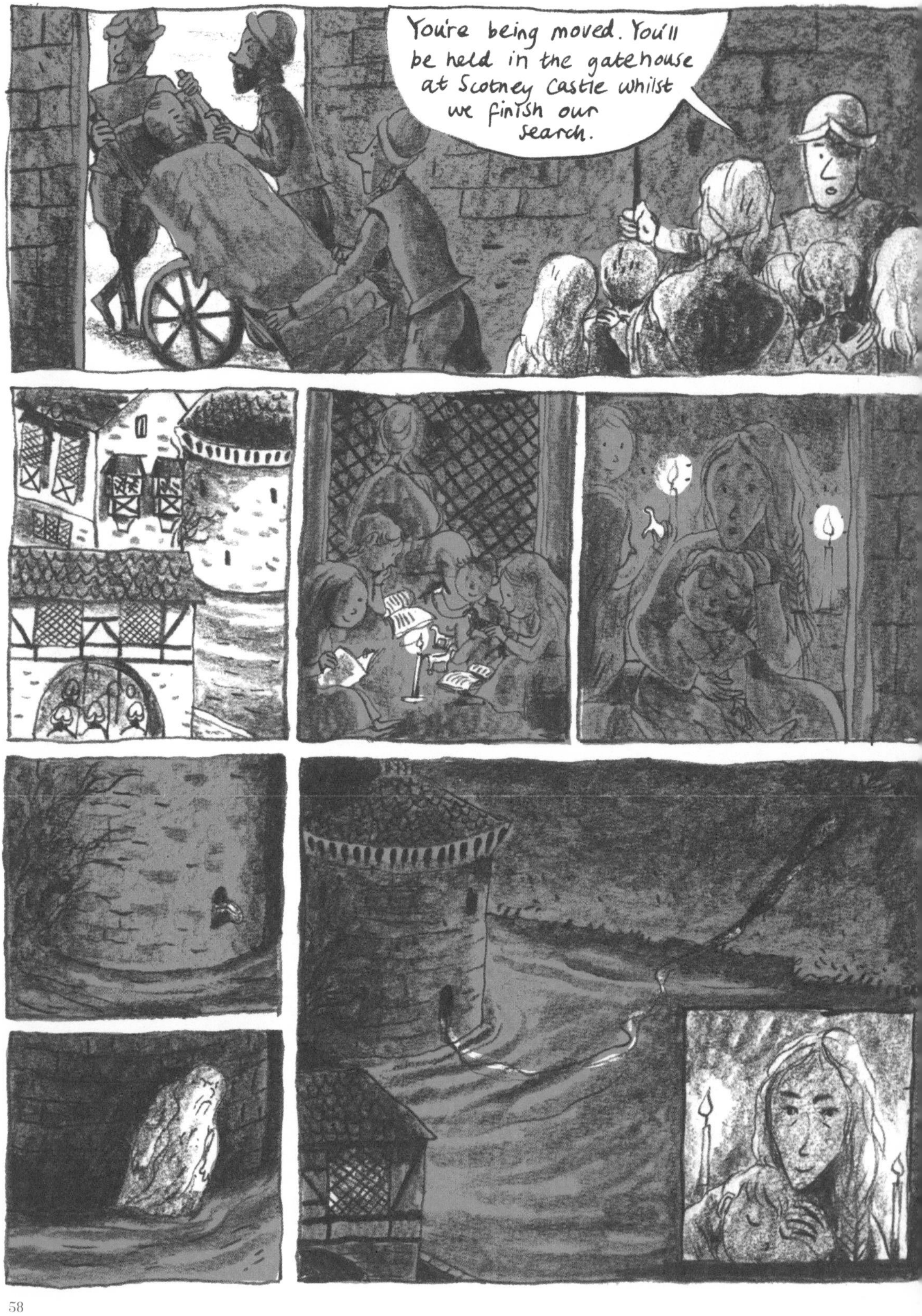
You're being moved. You'll be held in the gatehouse at Scotney Castle whilst we finish our search.

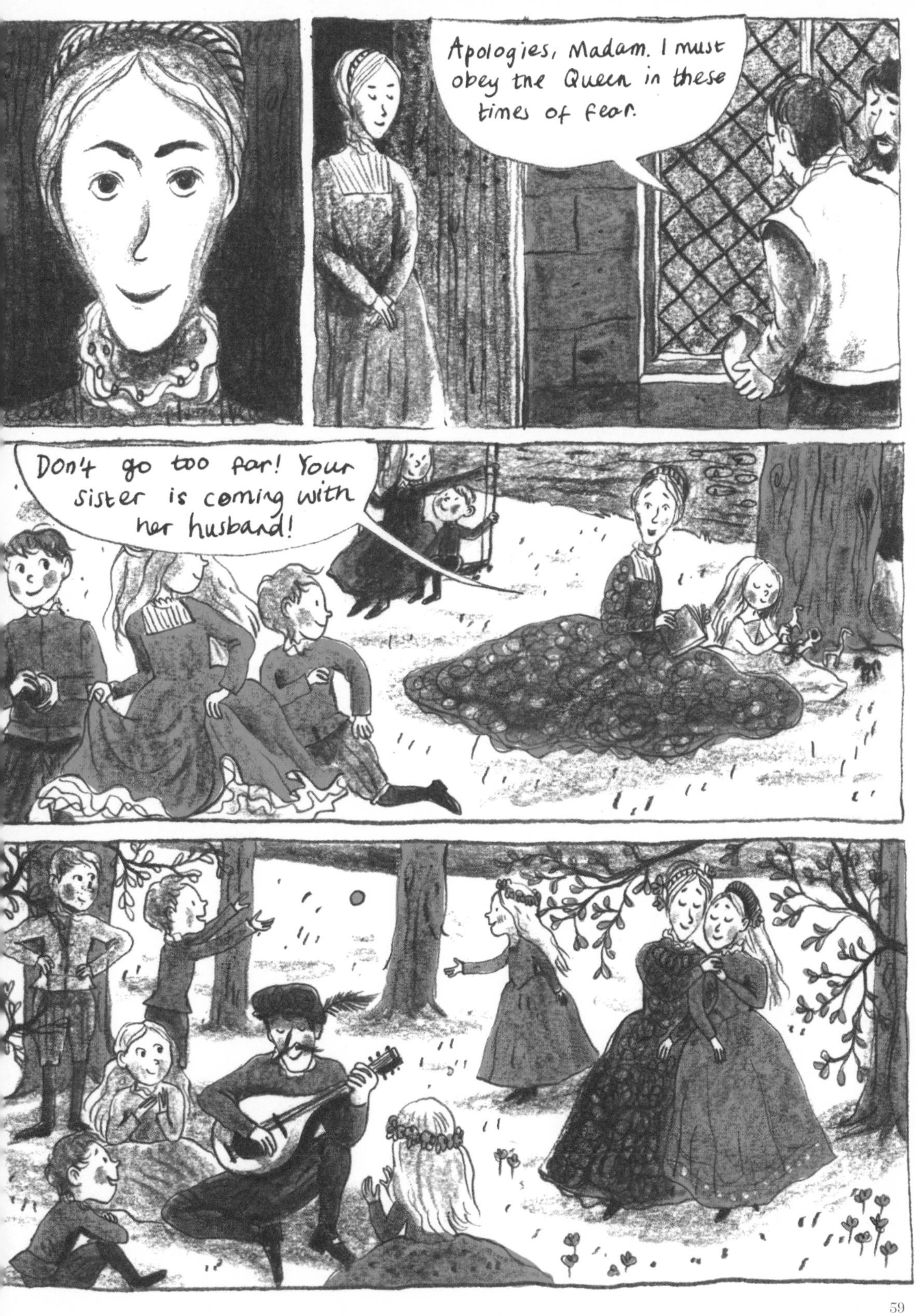
Apologies, Madam. I must obey the Queen in these times of fear.
Don't go too far! Your sister is coming with her husband!

THE PRIEST

Historical Context

1. This period is known as the English Reformation. The monarchy was in radical transition, and the religion of the country with it; from Church of England under Henry VIII, the country became briefly Protestant under Edward VI, Catholic under Mary I, and then Protestant again under Elizabeth I. These four changes to the accepted religion of the country happened within the space of just 11 years.

2. Catholic families suddenly found themselves on the end of violent persecution under Elizabeth, who was angry with the Pope for refusing to accept her as Queen; she regarded all Catholics as traitors not to be tolerated. This presented Catholics with the choice of remaining loyal to their church or to their country, and for priests it meant a life on the run or facing a gruesome death for treason.

3. It was a time of immense fear, full of plots, intrigues and conspiracies involving the highest levels of society. Brutal executions were commonplace and nobody was exempt. The people had seen King Henry VIII execute his own Queens, Mary I burn hundreds of people at the stake – commoners, nobles and clergymen alike – and Elizabeth frequently ordering people to be executed (including her own cousin, Mary Queen of Scots!).

Factual Background at Scotney Castle

1. In this period, the family who owned Scotney Castle were devout Catholics. Thomas Darell II inherited the castle in September 1558 with Mary I on the throne, however, Mary died in November the same year and with her, England ceased to be a Catholic nation. Elizabeth I came to the throne and forced England to become a Protestant nation. Those like the Darell family, who continued to adhere to Catholicism, suffered religious persecution.

2. In 1563 Protestant poet and writer, Barnabe Googe, sought to marry Thomas' daughter, Mary Darell. Thomas resisted the marriage, refusing to give consent, and though he could not openly say this was on religious grounds it is quite likely the reason. However, Barnabe Googe was a relative of Queen Elizabeth's chief advisor, Sir William Cecil, who ordered the Archbishop of Canterbury to intervene. Mary Darell was forcibly removed from the Darell household until her father relented, which he quickly did; there was no telling what would happen if Thomas continued to resist the marriage.

3. The Darell family's Catholic background must have been known, because in 1591 a celebrated Catholic priest arrived unexpectedly at the castle seeking refuge. The family took him in, and hid him in concealed areas within the castle. This was an enormous risk, and one which stands as testament to the strength of the family's beliefs and possibly their resentment towards the monarchy for the forced marriage of their daughter.

4. The priest remained with the family and was not looked for until 1597 when Justices of the Peace raided the castle. Records show the Darell family and their servants were sent to Newgate Prison and held there for roughly a year, with one "Mistress Darell" being allowed to leave to deliver a child at Scotney during this time. Thomas Darell died in prison in 1598.

5. The Justices did not find the priest, but raided the house again one year later, confining the family to a single room over the gatehouse whilst they searched the property. This time, the priest escaped by jumping into the moat and swimming to freedom whilst his servant distracted the Justices by shouting that their horses were being stolen. The priest was never seen again.

Darell Family Tree

The Stuart, Commonwealth and Hanoverian Eras

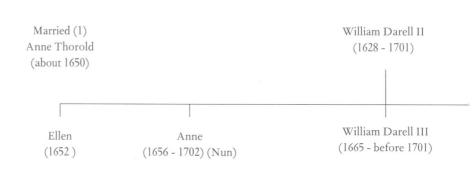

Married (1)
Anne Thorold
(about 1650)

William Darell II
(1628 - 1701)

Ellen
(1652)

Anne
(1656 - 1702) (Nun)

William Darell III
(1665 - before 1701)

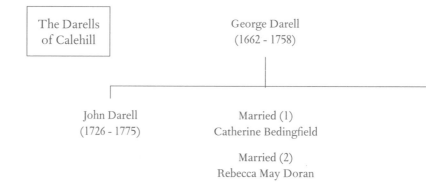

The Darells of Calehill

George Darell
(1662 - 1758)

John Darell
(1726 - 1775)

Married (1)
Catherine Bedingfield

Married (2)
Rebecca May Doran

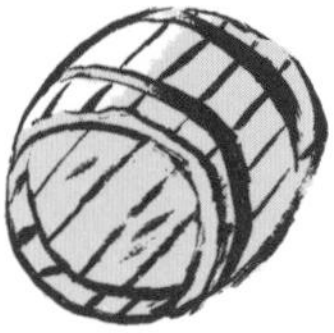

NOTE:

This information has been derived from various early documents and we cannot be sure of the accuracy

Married (2)
Elizabeth Warren
(in about 1664)

Thomas Darell
(1668 - 1710)

Arthur Darell
(1669 - 1720?)

Mary (1668 - 1750) (Nun)
Lucy (1677)
Margaret (1679 - 1761) (Nun)

Married
Mary Lowe
(about 1687)

Catherine
(1737 - 1802) (Nun)

—— Persons marked red feature in the story 'The Smuggler'

THE SMUGGLER

by William Exley

With the decline of the Kentish Iron Industry and the
tax increases to fund arms for the Jacobite Rebellion in
Scotland and wars in Europe, large numbers of the local
population became involved in the smuggling trade.
In 1710 the castle estate unexpectedly passed into the
hands of Arthur Darell when his older brother died.
Though part of the gentry, Arthur was reputed to be
involved in smuggling with the local gangs in the area.
Until, after reportedly killing a Revenue Officer, he
suddenly died in 1720. Yet, 200 years later, when the
family coffins were moved at the local churchyard, one
was found to be full of rocks…

Georgian Era
The Georgian Smuggling Boom
- 1720 -

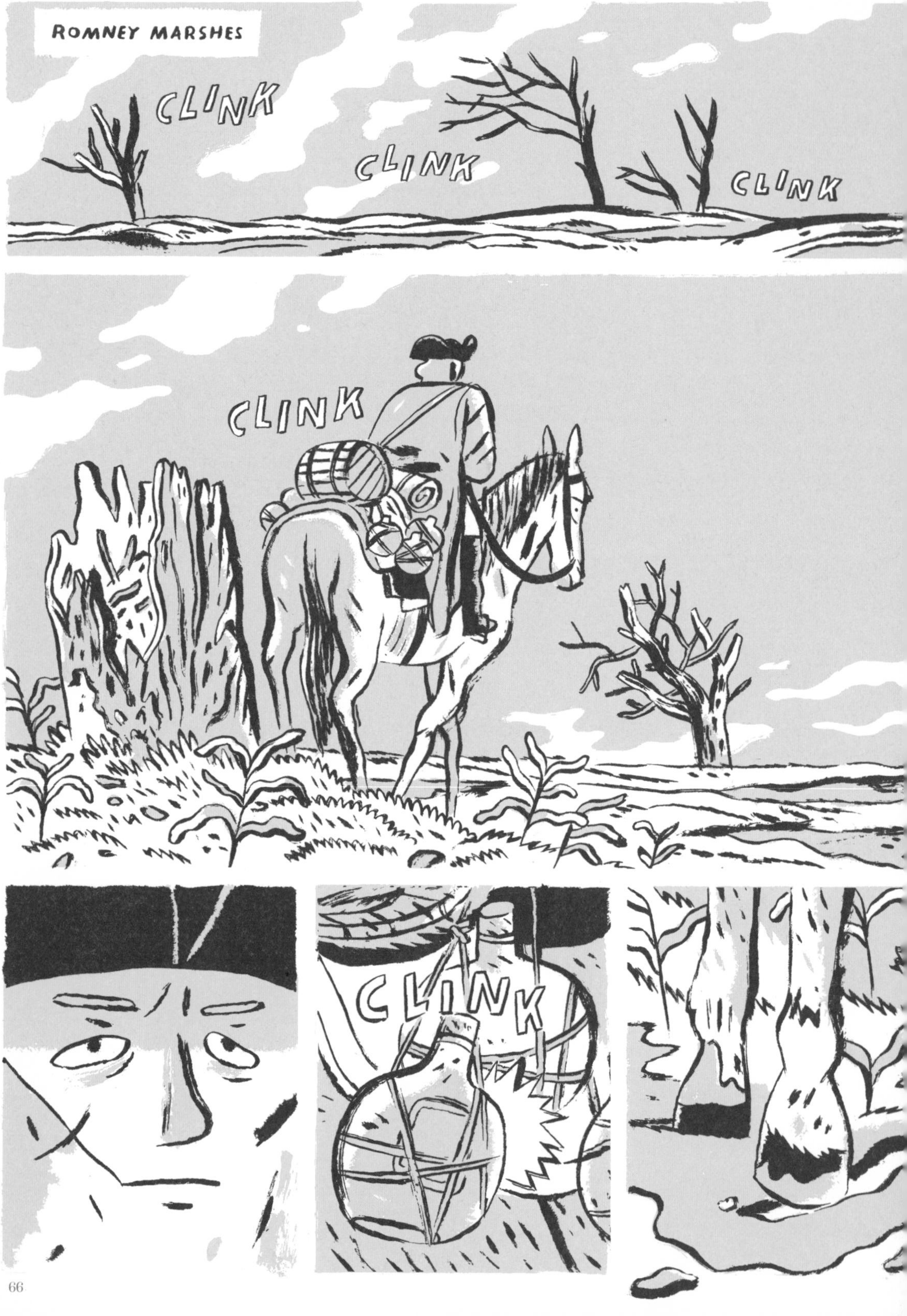
ROMNEY MARSHES
CLINK
CLINK
CLINK
CLINK
CLINK

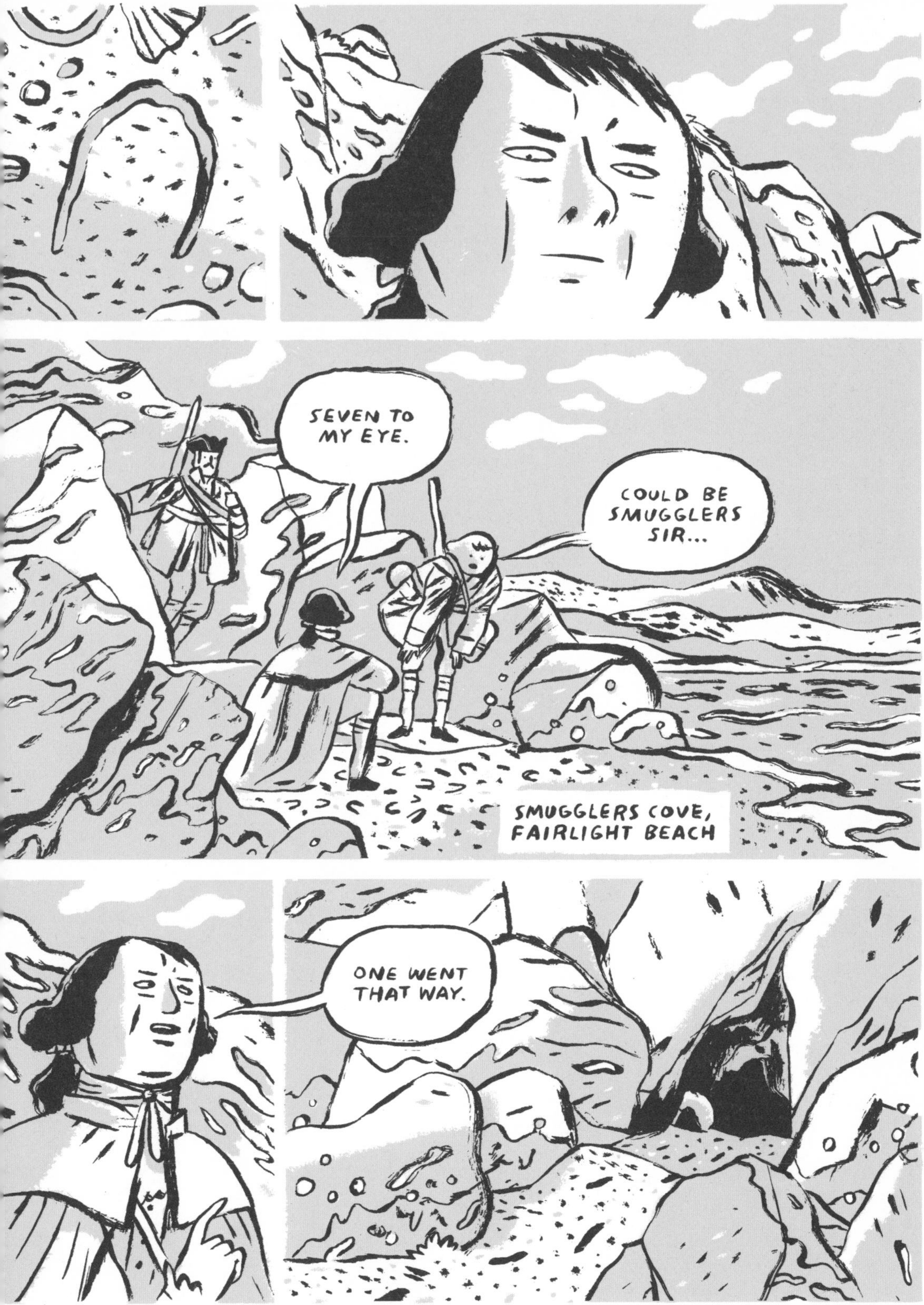
SEVEN TO MY EYE.
COULD BE SMUGGLERS SIR...
SMUGGLERS COVE, FAIRLIGHT BEACH
ONE WENT THAT WAY.

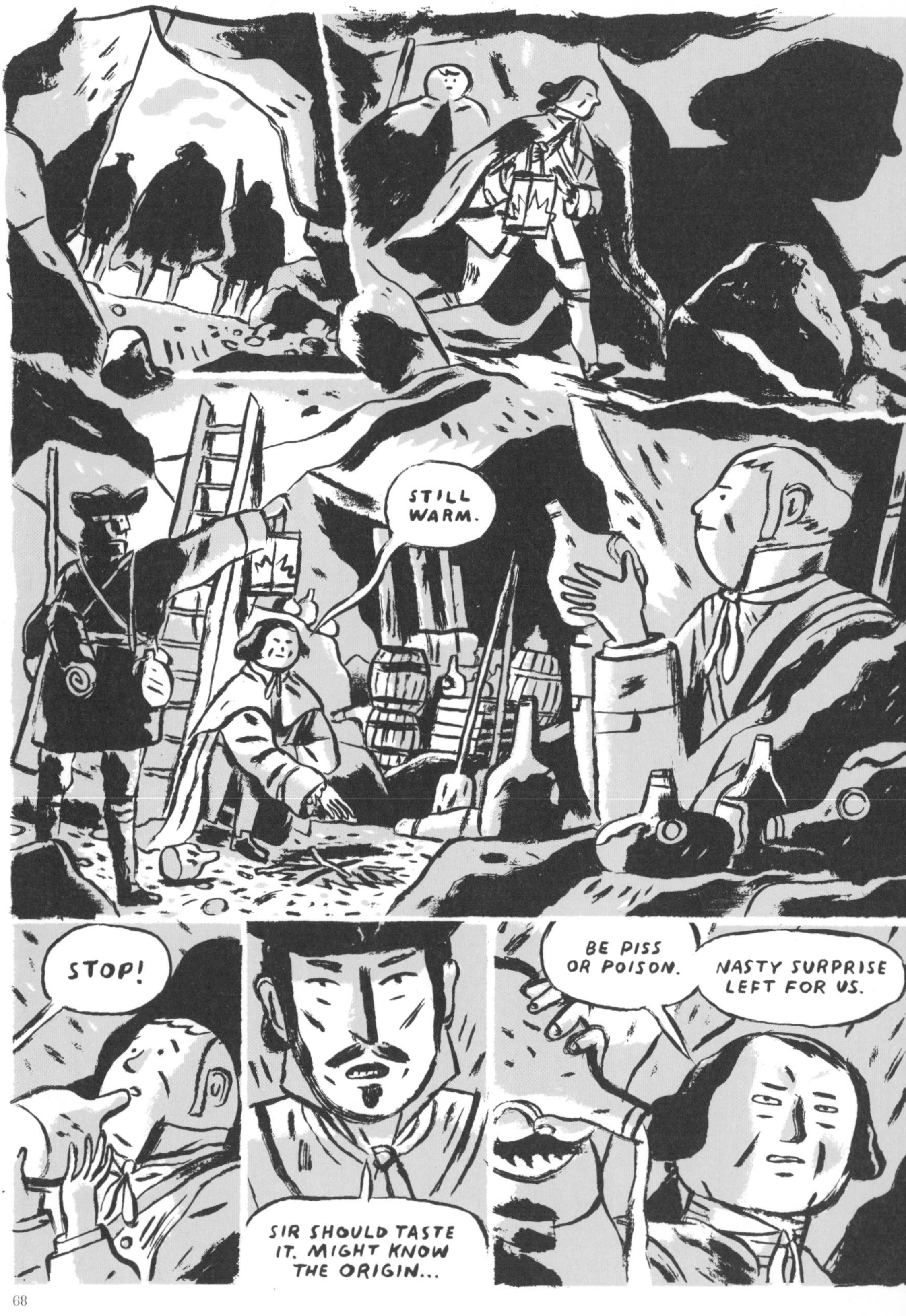
STILL WARM.
STOP!
SIR SHOULD TASTE IT. MIGHT KNOW THE ORIGIN...
BE PISS OR POISON.
NASTY SURPRISE LEFT FOR US.

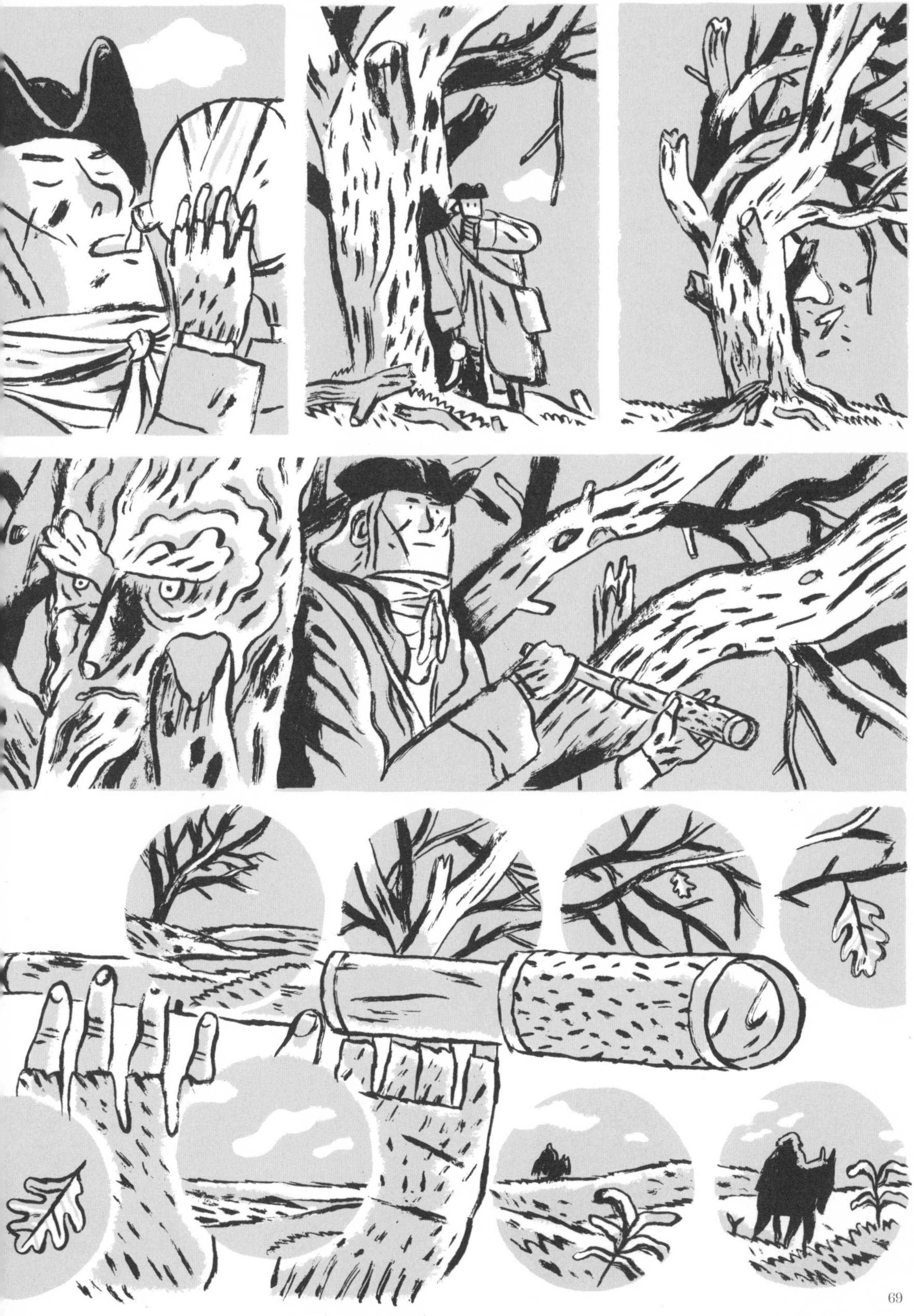

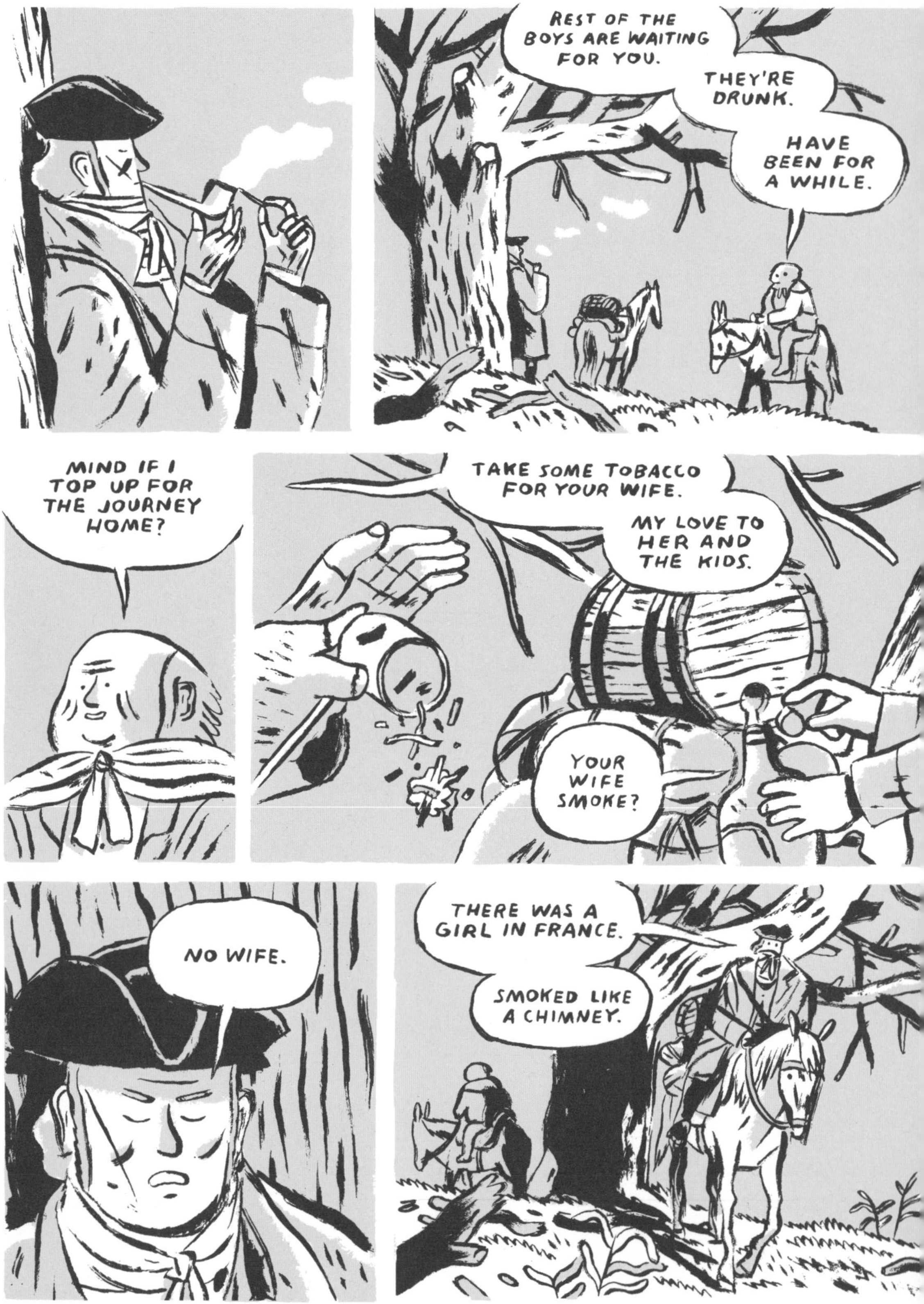
REST OF THE BOYS ARE WAITING FOR YOU.
THEY'RE DRUNK.
HAVE BEEN FOR A WHILE.
MIND IF I TOP UP FOR THE JOURNEY HOME?
TAKE SOME TOBACCO FOR YOUR WIFE.
MY LOVE TO HER AND THE KIDS.
YOUR WIFE SMOKE?
NO WIFE.
THERE WAS A GIRL IN FRANCE.
SMOKED LIKE A CHIMNEY.

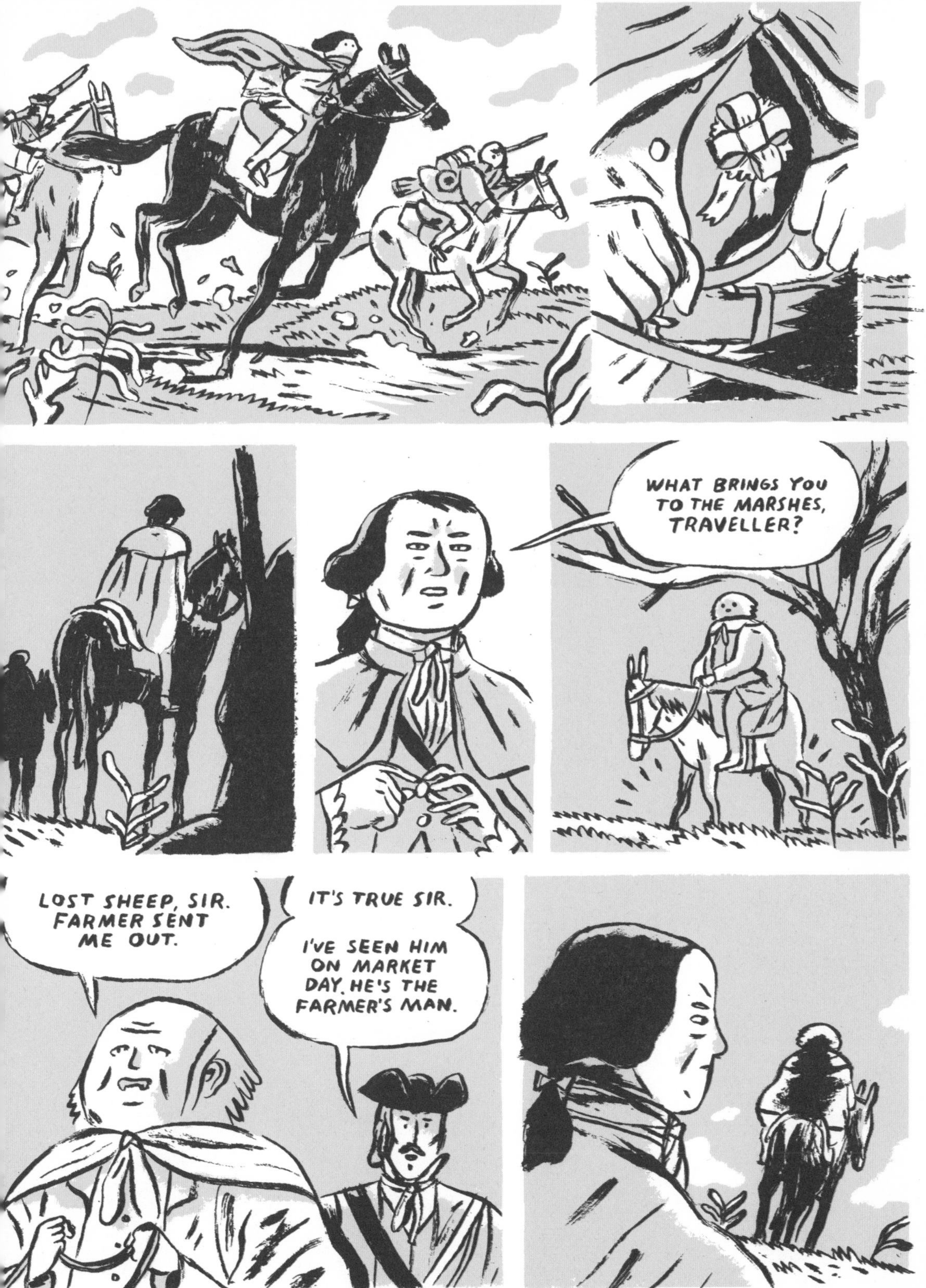
WHAT BRINGS YOU TO THE MARSHES, TRAVELLER?
LOST SHEEP, SIR. FARMER SENT ME OUT.
IT'S TRUE SIR.
I'VE SEEN HIM ON MARKET DAY. HE'S THE FARMER'S MAN.

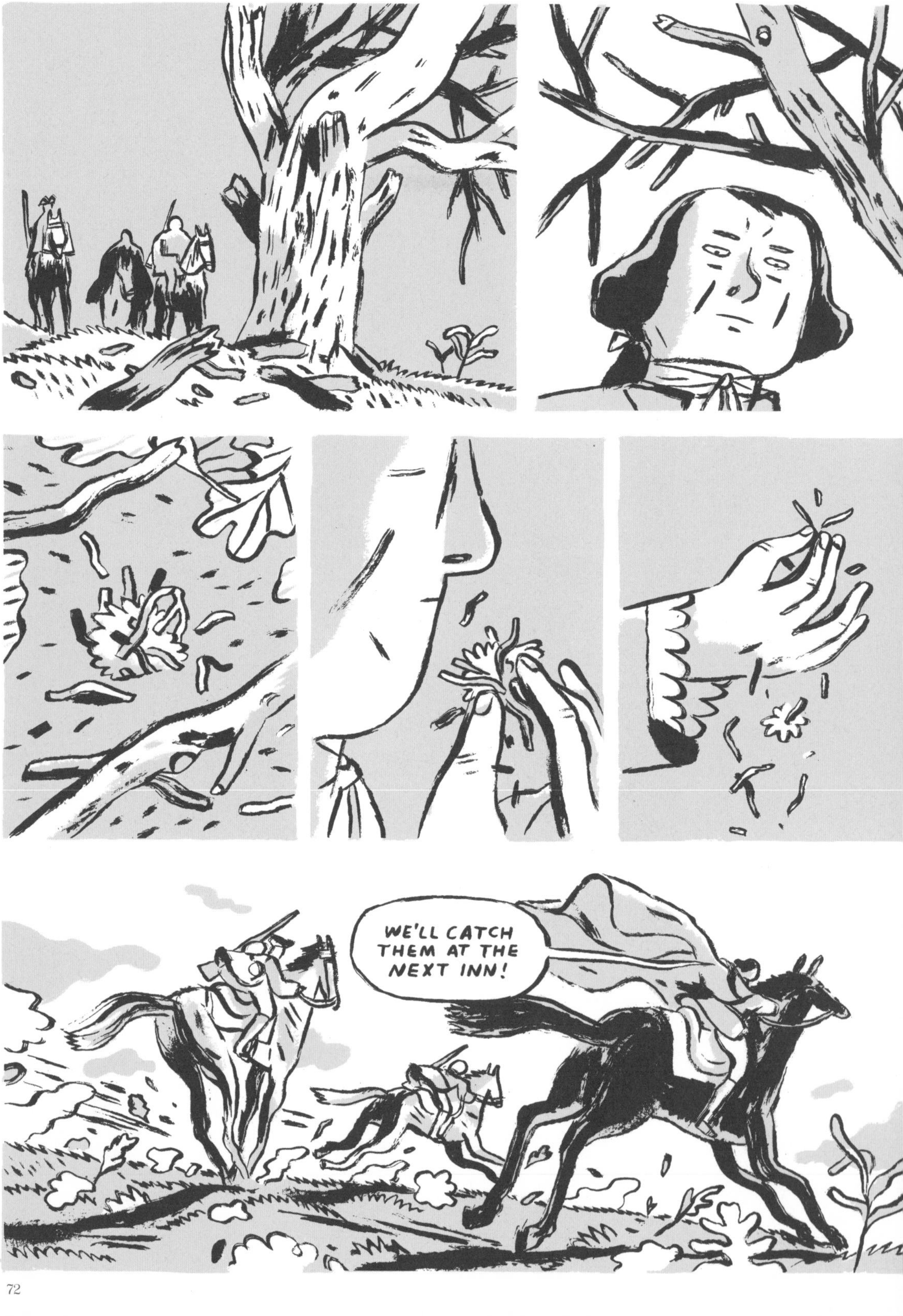
WE'LL CATCH THEM AT THE NEXT INN!

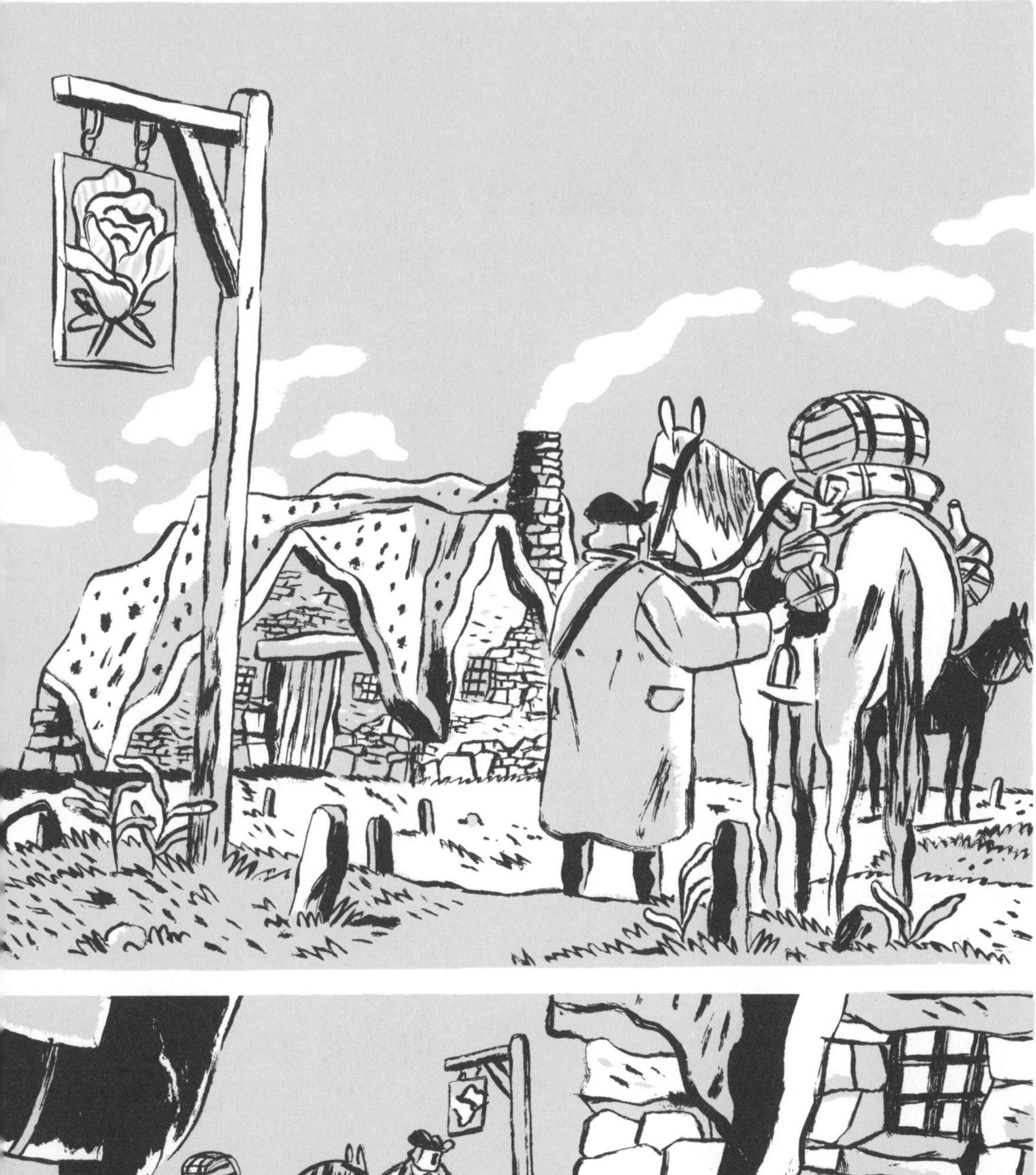

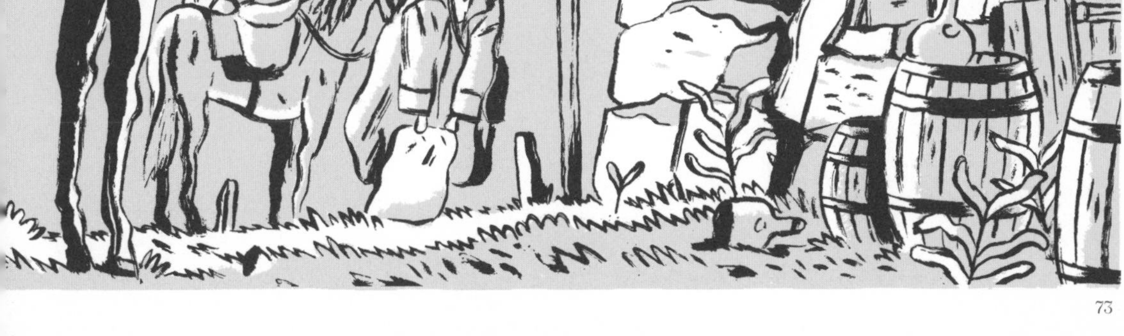

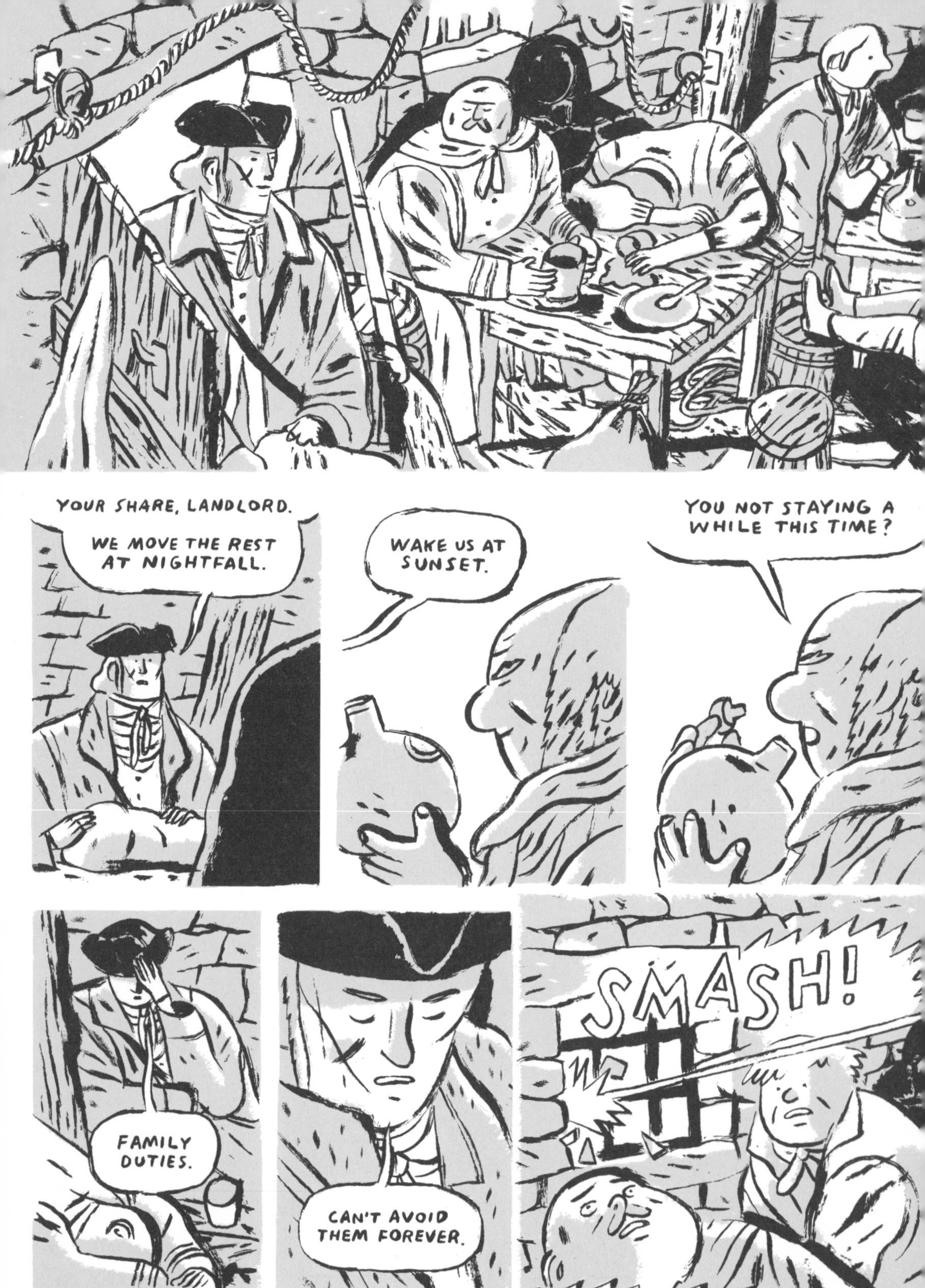

YOUR SHARE, LANDLORD.
WE MOVE THE REST AT NIGHTFALL.
WAKE US AT SUNSET.
YOU NOT STAYING A WHILE THIS TIME?
FAMILY DUTIES.
CAN'T AVOID THEM FOREVER.
SMASH!

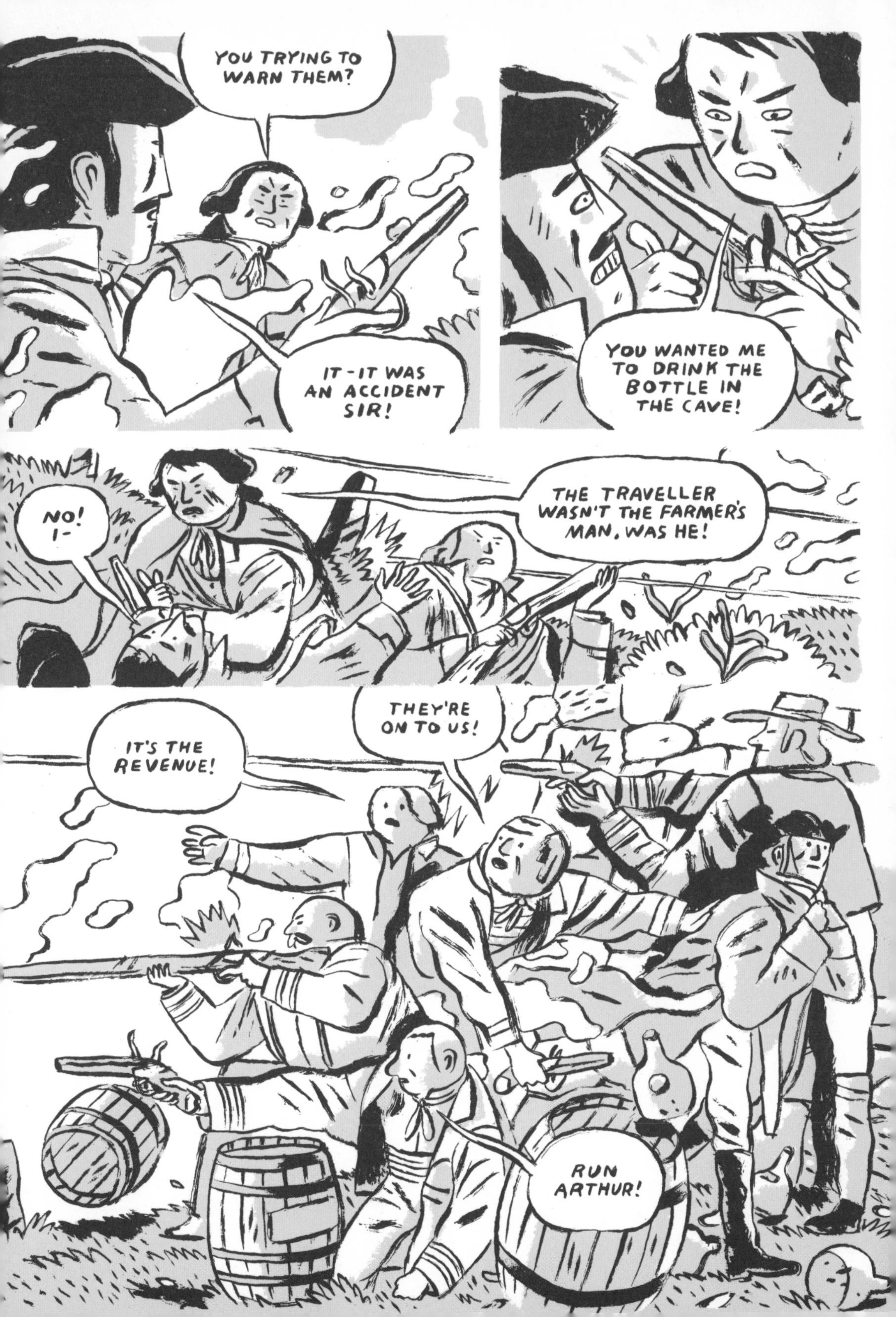
YOU TRYING TO WARN THEM?
IT-IT WAS AN ACCIDENT SIR!
YOU WANTED ME TO DRINK THE BOTTLE IN THE CAVE!
NO! I-
THE TRAVELLER WASN'T THE FARMER'S MAN, WAS HE!
IT'S THE REVENUE!
THEY'RE ON TO US!
RUN ARTHUR!

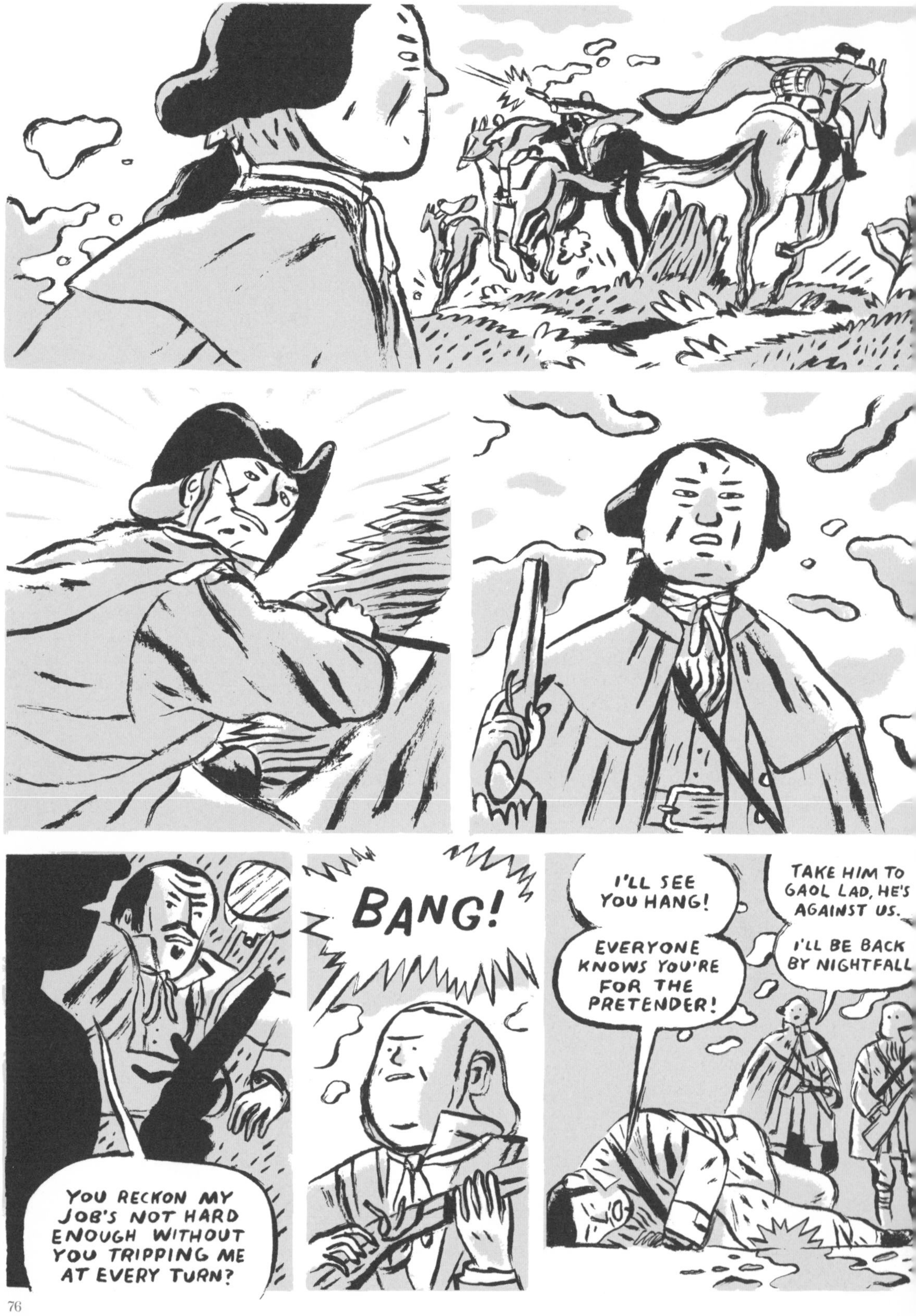
YOU RECKON MY JOB'S NOT HARD ENOUGH WITHOUT YOU TRIPPING ME AT EVERY TURN?
BANG!
I'LL SEE YOU HANG!
EVERYONE KNOWS YOU'RE FOR THE PRETENDER!
TAKE HIM TO GAOL LAD, HE'S AGAINST US.
I'LL BE BACK BY NIGHTFALL

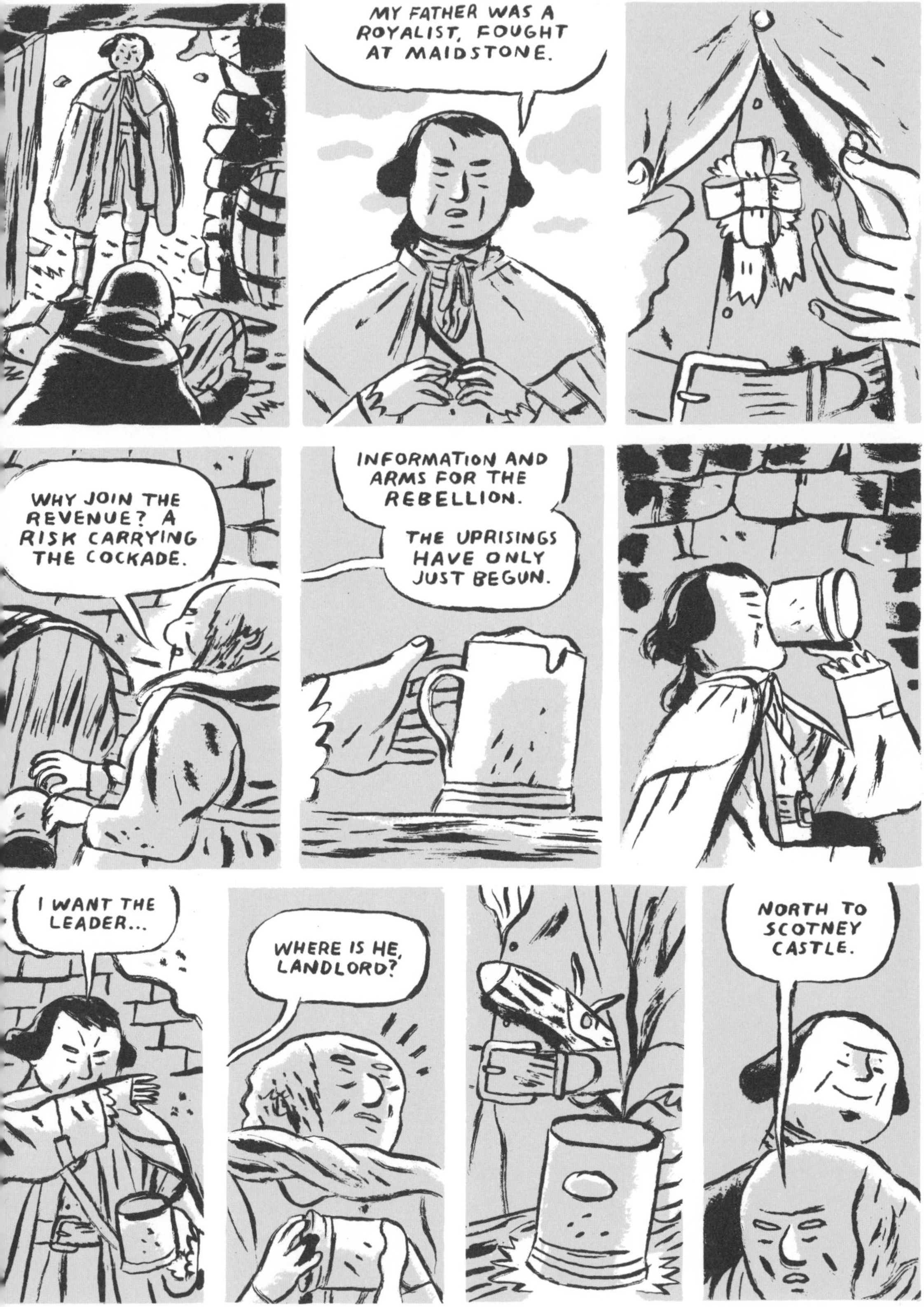
MY FATHER WAS A ROYALIST, FOUGHT AT MAIDSTONE.
WHY JOIN THE REVENUE? A RISK CARRYING THE COCKADE.
INFORMATION AND ARMS FOR THE REBELLION.
THE UPRISINGS HAVE ONLY JUST BEGUN.
I WANT THE LEADER...
WHERE IS HE, LANDLORD?
NORTH TO SCOTNEY CASTLE.

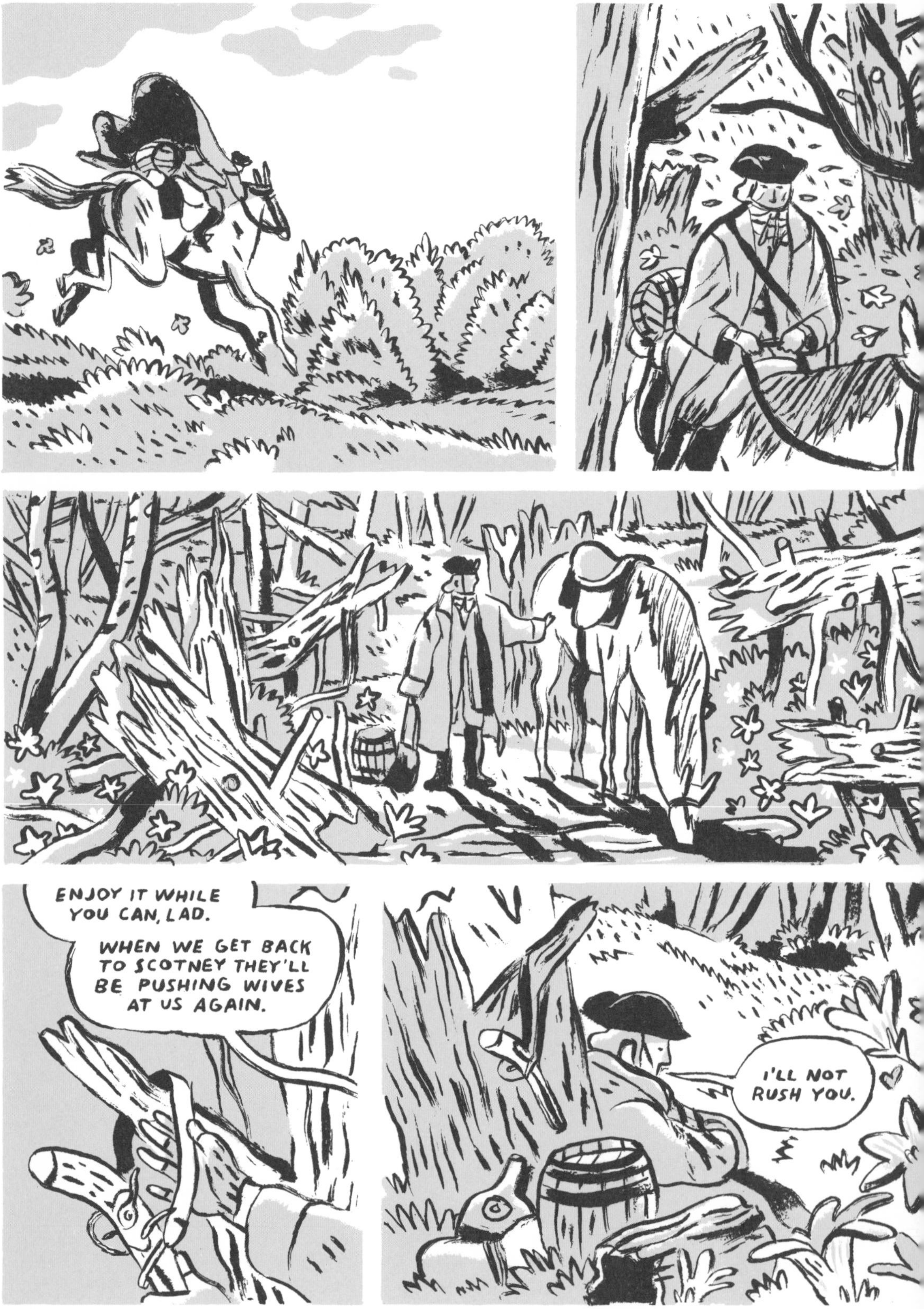
ENJOY IT WHILE YOU CAN, LAD.
WHEN WE GET BACK TO SCOTNEY THEY'LL BE PUSHING WIVES AT US AGAIN.
I'LL NOT RUSH YOU.

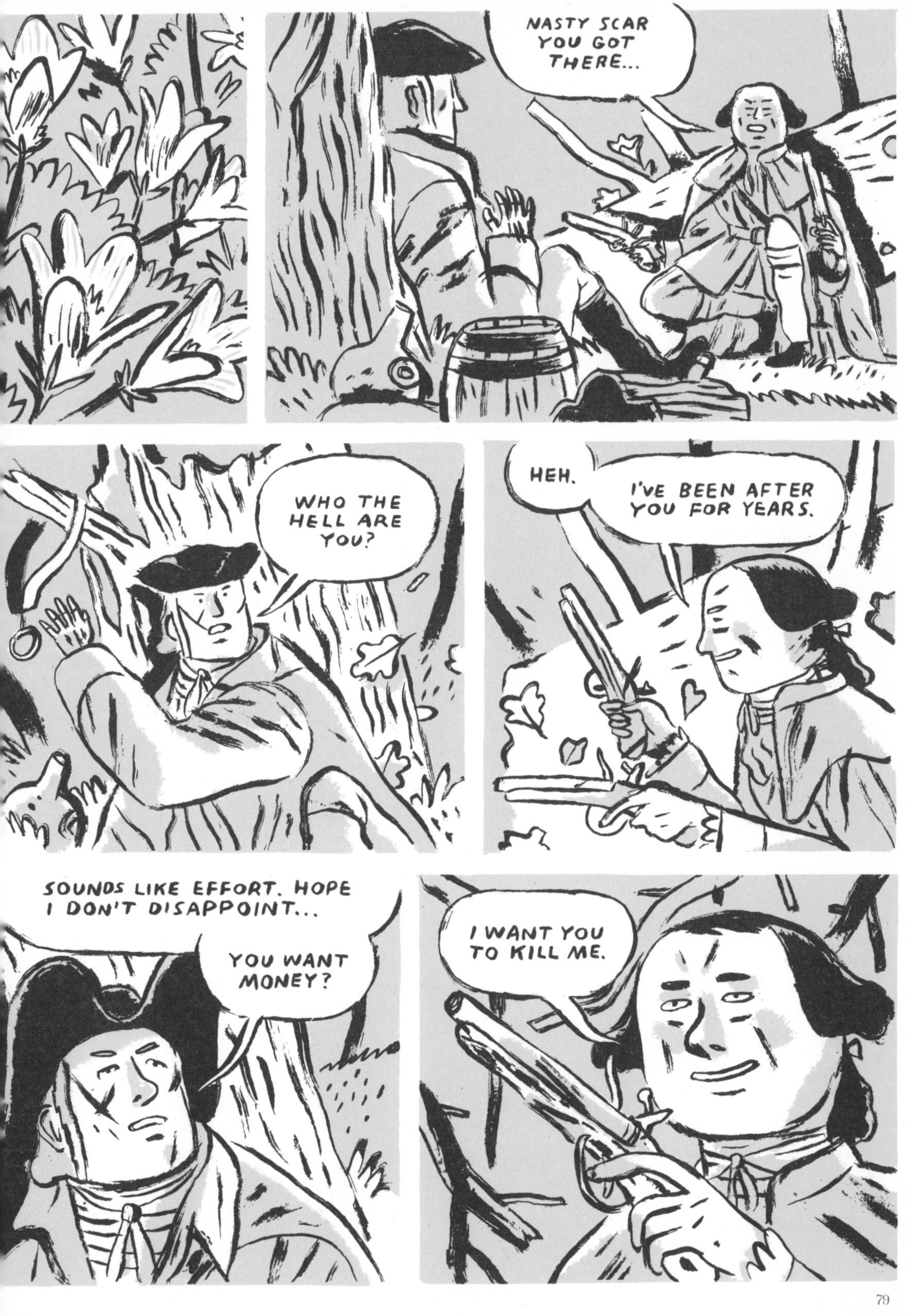
NASTY SCAR YOU GOT THERE...
WHO THE HELL ARE YOU?
HEH.
I'VE BEEN AFTER YOU FOR YEARS.
SOUNDS LIKE EFFORT. HOPE I DON'T DISAPPOINT...
YOU WANT MONEY?
I WANT YOU TO KILL ME.

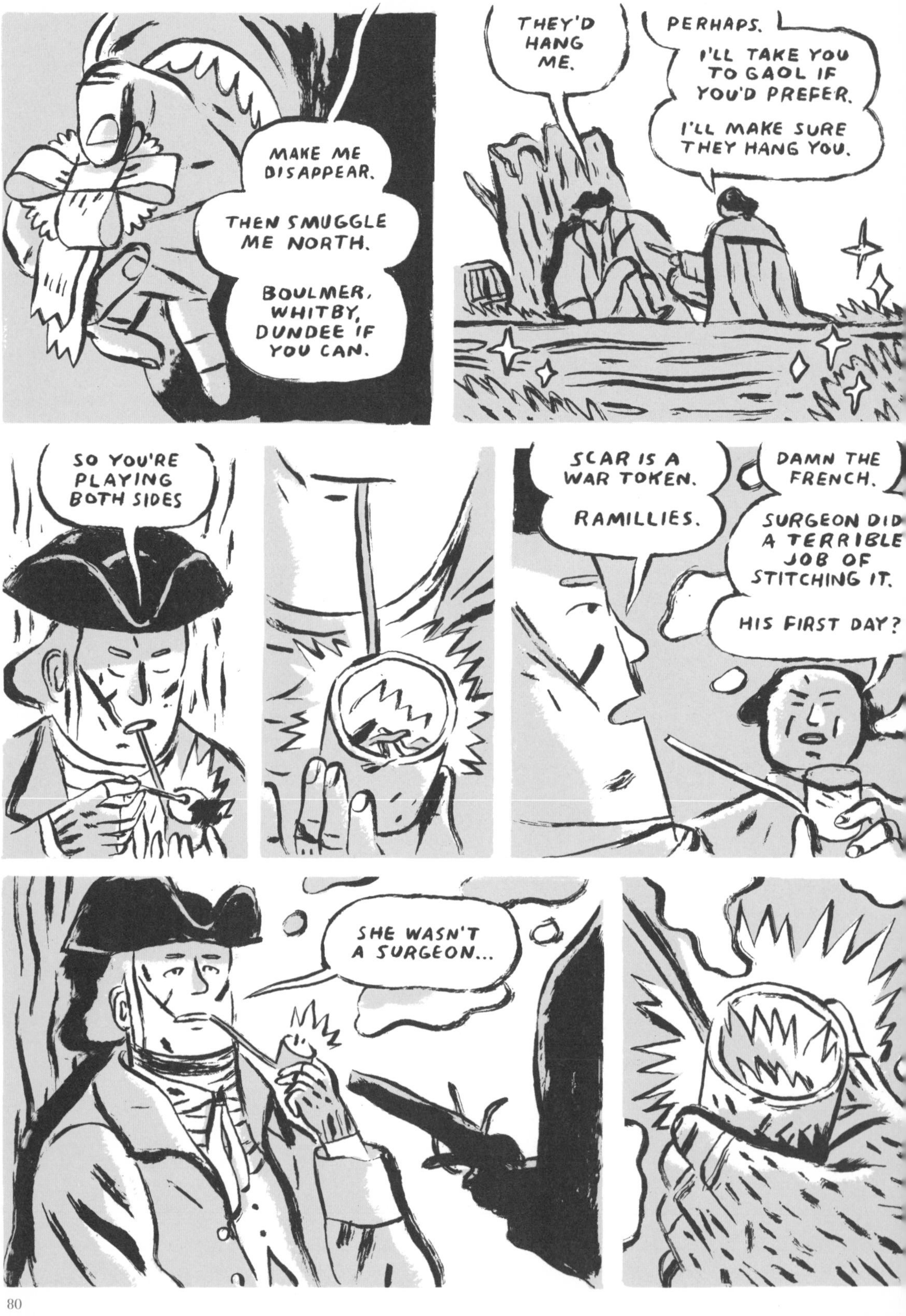
MAKE ME DISAPPEAR.
THEN SMUGGLE ME NORTH.
BOULMER, WHITBY, DUNDEE IF YOU CAN.
THEY'D HANG ME.
PERHAPS.
I'LL TAKE YOU TO GAOL IF YOU'D PREFER.
I'LL MAKE SURE THEY HANG YOU.
SO YOU'RE PLAYING BOTH SIDES
SCAR IS A WAR TOKEN.
RAMILLIES.
DAMN THE FRENCH.
SURGEON DID A TERRIBLE JOB OF STITCHING IT.
HIS FIRST DAY?
SHE WASN'T A SURGEON...

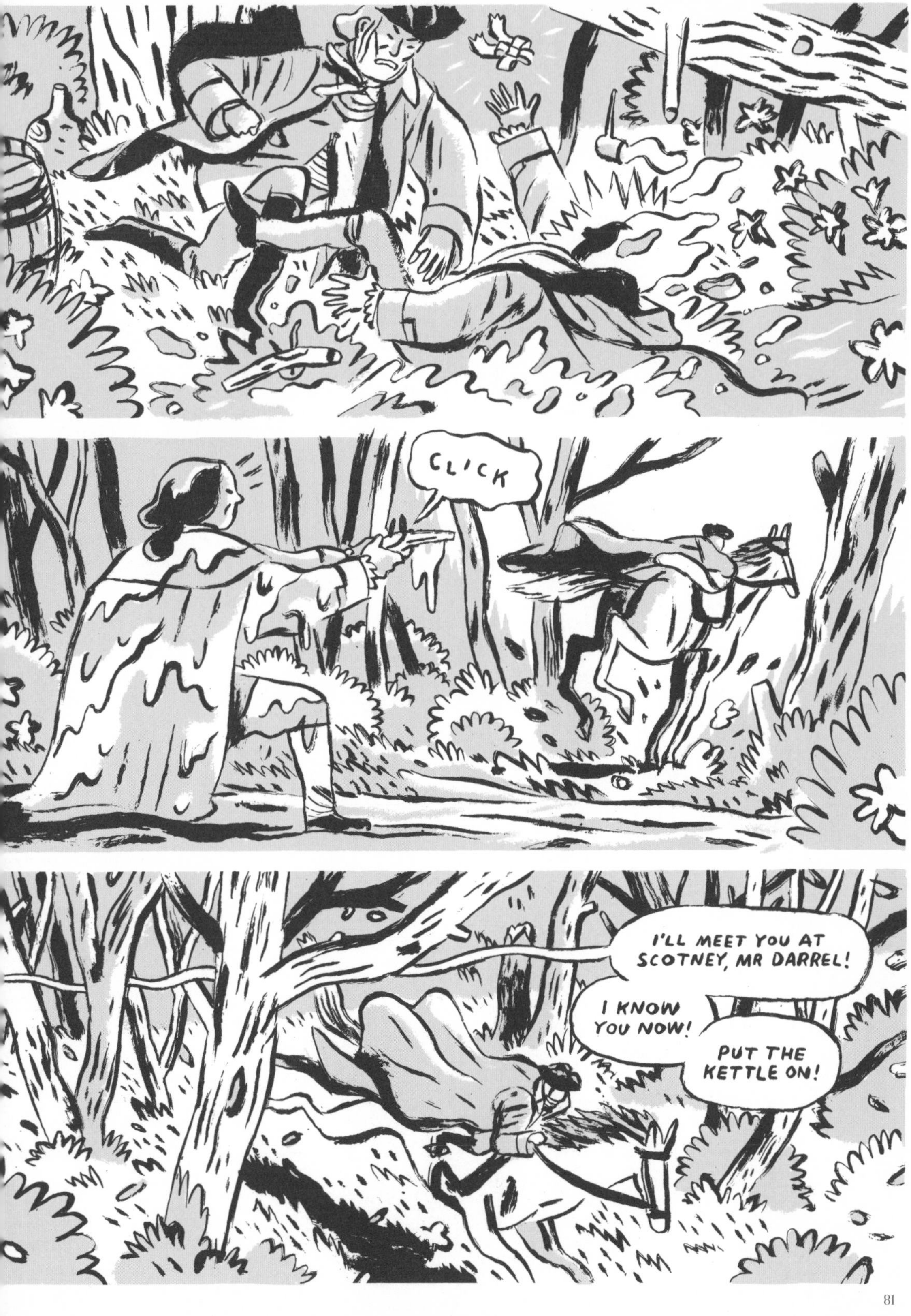
CLICK
I'LL MEET YOU AT SCOTNEY, MR DARREL!
I KNOW YOU NOW!
PUT THE KETTLE ON!

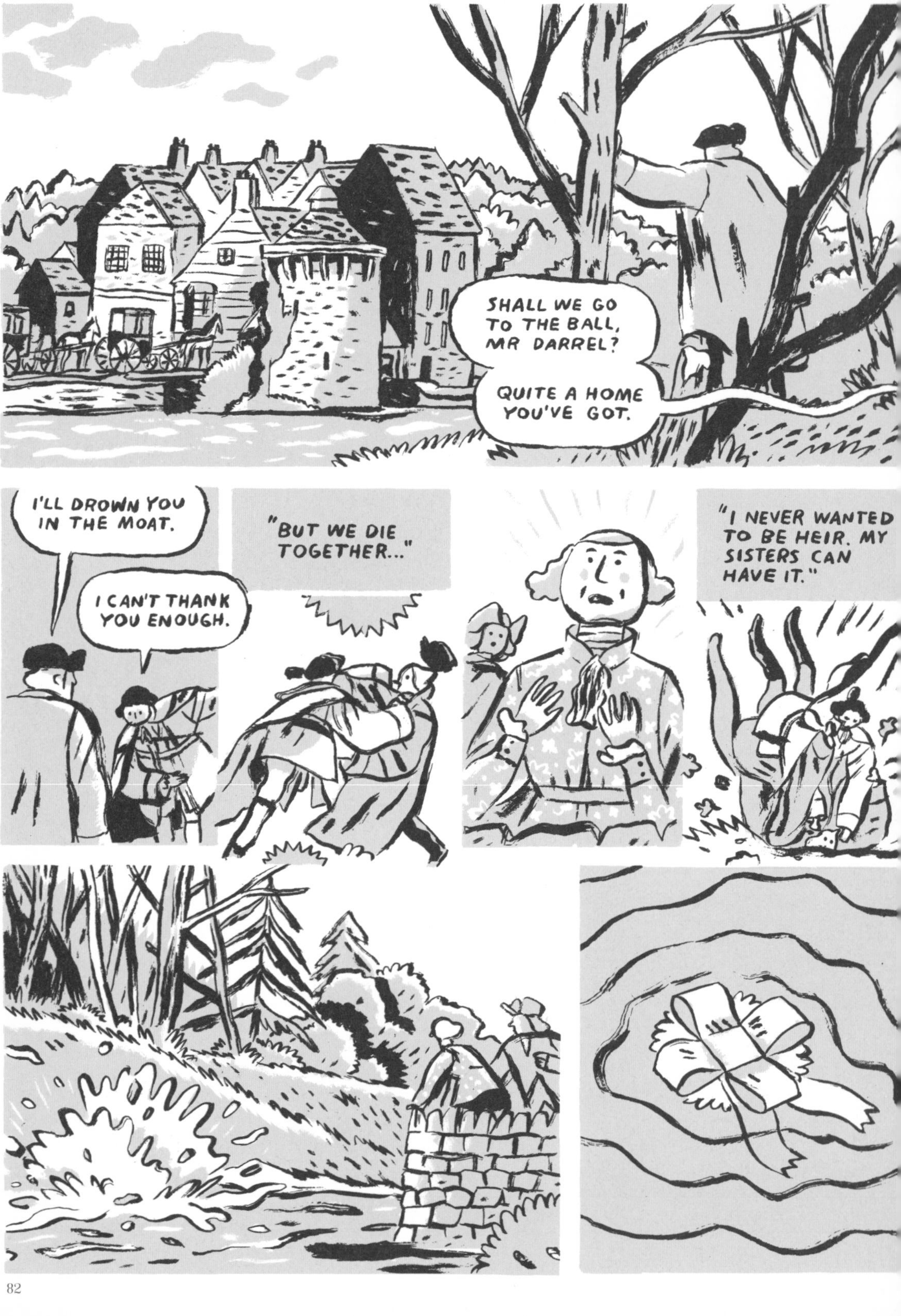
SHALL WE GO TO THE BALL, MR DARREL?
QUITE A HOME YOU'VE GOT.
I'LL DROWN YOU IN THE MOAT.
I CAN'T THANK YOU ENOUGH.
"BUT WE DIE TOGETHER..."
"I NEVER WANTED TO BE HEIR. MY SISTERS CAN HAVE IT."

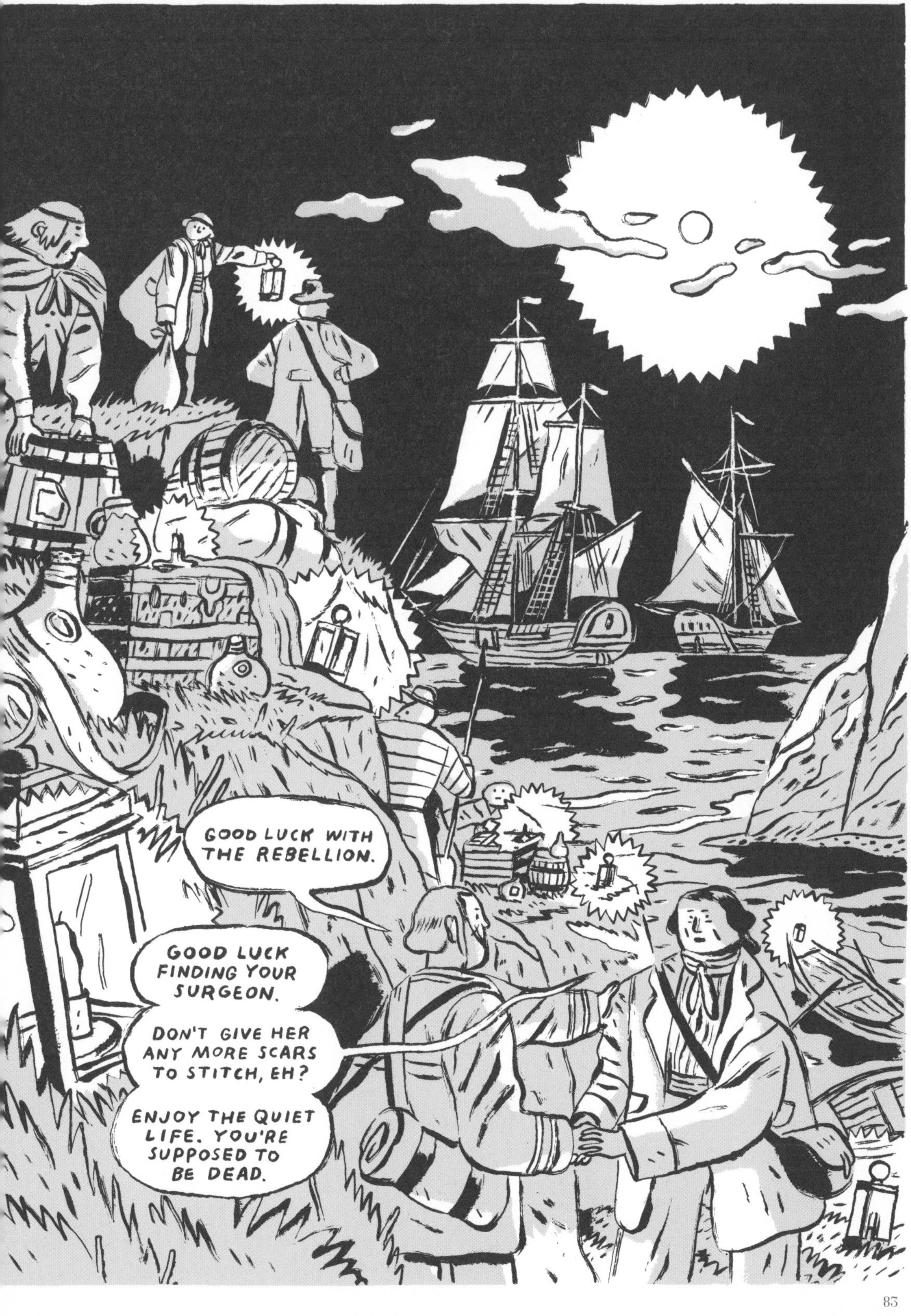
GOOD LUCK WITH THE REBELLION.
GOOD LUCK FINDING YOUR SURGEON.
DON'T GIVE HER ANY MORE SCARS TO STITCH, EH?
ENJOY THE QUIET LIFE. YOU'RE SUPPOSED TO BE DEAD.

THE SMUGGLER

Historical Context

1. With the decline of the Kentish Iron Industry and the tax increases to fund arms for the Jacobite Rebellion in Scotland and wars in Europe, large numbers of the local population became involved in the smuggling trade. In the 18th century, illegal trade across England's coast grew at a prodigious rate. What had previously been simple small-scale evasion of duty turned into an industry of astonishing proportions, syphoning money abroad, and channelling huge volumes of contraband into the southern counties of England.

2. Even by modern standards, the quantities of imported goods are extraordinary. It was not unheard of for a smuggling trip to bring in 3,000 gallons of spirits. Illegally imported gin was sometimes so plentiful that the inhabitants of some Kentish villages were said to use it for cleaning their windows. And according to some contemporary estimates, ⅘ of all tea drunk in England had not paid duty.

3. Statistics like this are even more extraordinary when seen in the light of the time. Sailing ships brought the goods from the continent, and kegs and bales were man-handled – often up sheer cliffs. Carriers then transported the goods either in carts or caravans of ponies, or lashed the tubs to their own backs for a journey inland.

4. This extraordinary situation was not the result of some plan or a plot hatched in a smugglers' tunnel. Rather, it was a natural and inevitable result of punitive taxation imposed by a succession of governments, each more desperate than the last. As the 18th century progressed, the slice taken by the exchequer increased, sometimes by leaps and bounds.

Factual Background
at Scotney Castle

1. In 1710 the castle estate unexpectedly passed into the hands of Arthur Darell when his older brother died. He lived at the castle with his two sisters until his mysterious "death" in 1720. His sisters then fought a long legal battle with a distant male cousin over inheritance of the castle.

2. Though part of the gentry, Arthur was reputed to be involved in smuggling with the local gangs in the area. He would likely have smuggled wool out of Kent and East Sussex, crossing the channel to Calais to bring wine and spirits in. Smugglers who traded in wool were known as 'Owlers', and smuggling in the Kent/Sussex area reached its peak rather conveniently right around the same time that Arthur Darell inherited the castle. The secret chambers in the castle that had once been priest holes would have made convenient holding rooms for contraband awaiting transport to London; Scotney Castle is roughly halfway between the Kentish coast and London.

3. Smuggling was relatively non-violent to begin with; Revenue Men would usually be tied up and freed later, rather than murdered. However,

in 1720 Arthur Darell is said to have killed a Revenue Officer and dumped him in the castle moat. He was then forced to fake his own death to escape the law, and the legend follows that he attended his own funeral, standing at the back of the room wearing a hooded black cloak to disguise his features.

4. After Arthur's disappearance, the smuggling trade turned very violent with new gangs from Hawkhurst and Mayfield terrorising the local populace as well as brutally murdering and torturing the Revenue Men, who responded with similar violence.

5. 200 years later, in the early 1900s, the sexton at the local church where the Darell families are buried needed to rearrange the coffins to make more space. Arthur's coffin was unusually heavy and the lid was sealed shut with heavy iron nails. When prised open, it was found to be full of rocks. First-hand accounts of this detail, and the contemporary reports from the sexton himself, confirm it to be true.

HUSSEY FAMILY TREE
3rd family to take the castle

From the Victorian Era onwards

Edward Hussey
(1749 - 1816)

Married
Elizabeth-Sarah Bridge, only daughter and heir
of Robert Birdge of Bocking, Essex
(1775) (5 children)

Edward Hussey II
(1780 - 1817)

Married
Anne Jemmet
(1805)

Ellen Louisa
(1811 - 1820)
(died aged 9)

Edward Hussey III
(1807 - 1894)

Edward Windsor Hussey
(1855 - 1952)

William Clive Hussey
(1858 - 1929)

Gertrude Anne Hussey
(1861 - 1921)

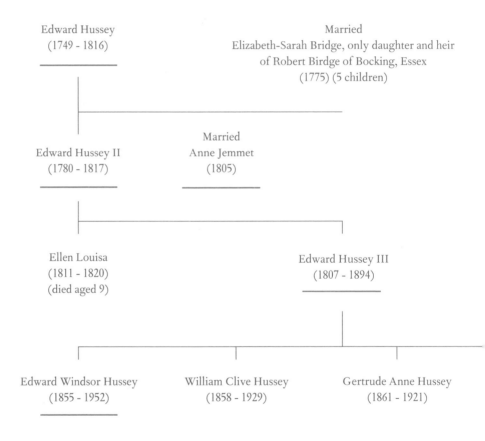

CLIVE FAMILY TREE
Married into the Hussey family

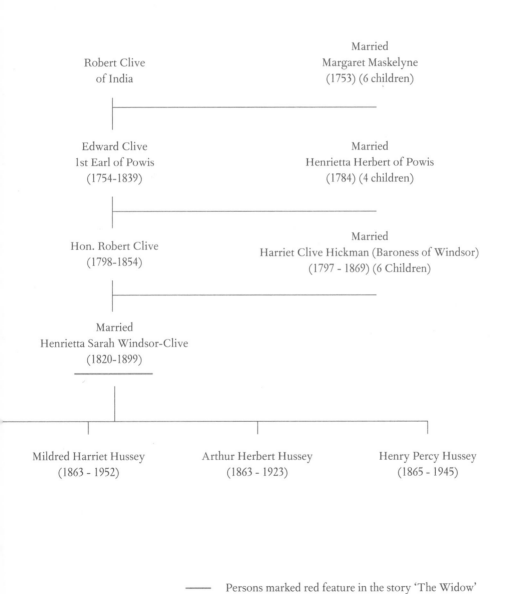

Robert Clive
of India

Married
Margaret Maskelyne
(1753) (6 children)

Edward Clive
1st Earl of Powis
(1754-1839)

Married
Henrietta Herbert of Powis
(1784) (4 children)

Hon. Robert Clive
(1798-1854)

Married
Harriet Clive Hickman (Baroness of Windsor)
(1797 - 1869) (6 Children)

Married
Henrietta Sarah Windsor-Clive
(1820-1899)

Mildred Harriet Hussey
(1863 - 1952)

Arthur Herbert Hussey
(1863 - 1923)

Henry Percy Hussey
(1865 - 1945)

—— Persons marked red feature in the story 'The Widow'

THE WIDOW
by Becky Palmer

Recent scientific advances meant that wealthy people were more interested in, and able to influence, their health than ever before. When the owner of Scotney Castle, Edward Hussey I, committed suicide with a blunderbuss in 1816, and his adult son Edward Hussey II died of a long-term illness, his widow Anne and ten year old Edward Hussey III were left alone. Anne took Edward III away, believing the old castle to be a deeply unhealthy place. However, a decade later, an adult Edward III returned to recover his inheritance…

Victorian Era
The age of science & progress
- 1819 to 1855 -

Will father ever be allowed back in our carriage?

If he ever gets well. Come away from the window, you'll fall out.

Perhaps your grandfather will play with you if he's not in one of his moods.

I hate going to Scotney, it's damp and scary and Grandfather is always miserable.

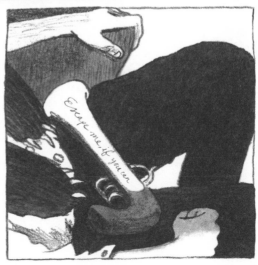

Escape me if you can

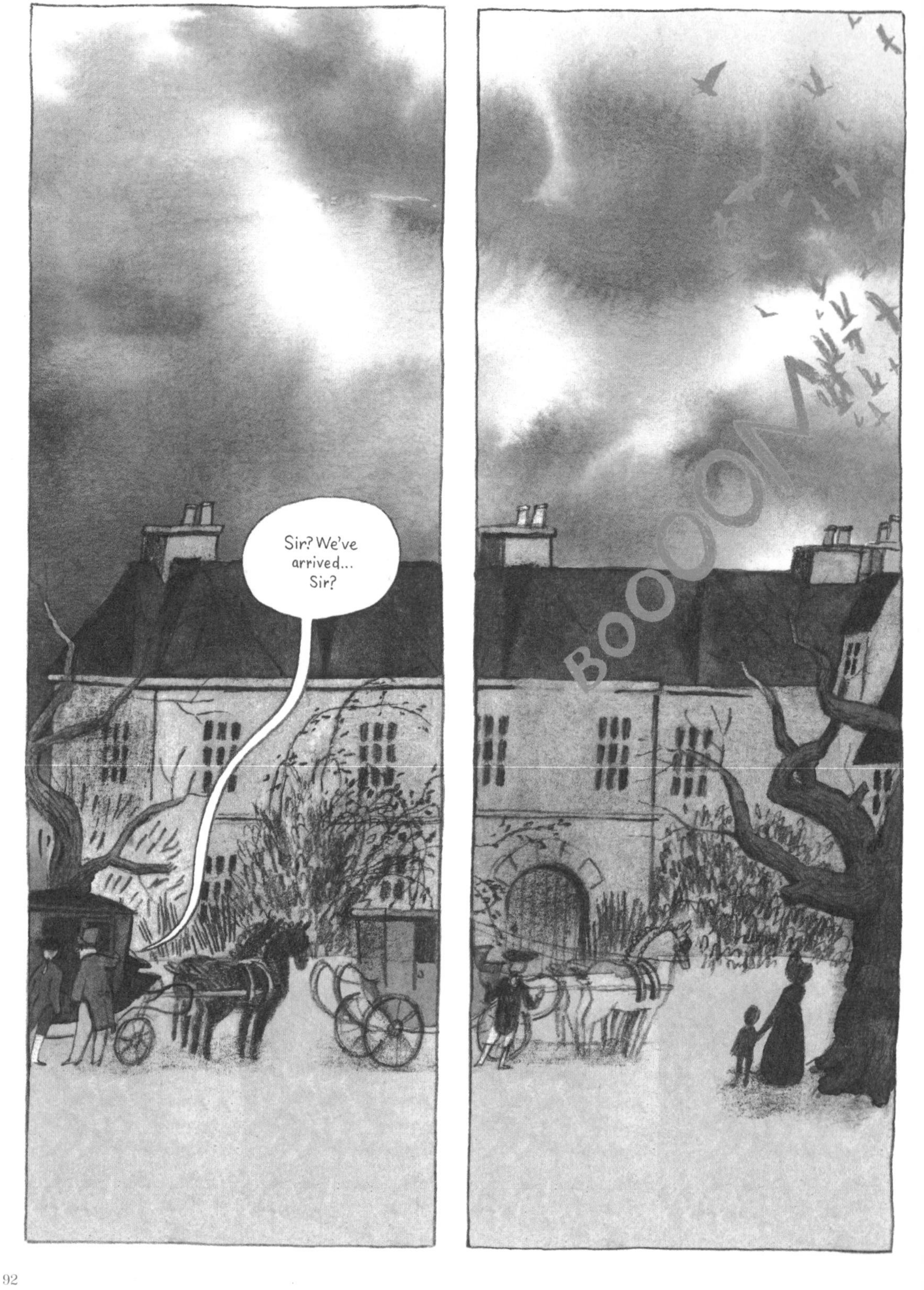
Sir? We've arrived... Sir?
BOOOOM

Fetch my husband!
Ma'am...
...your husband...
The cold air here.
The jarring potholes.
His lungs finally gave out.

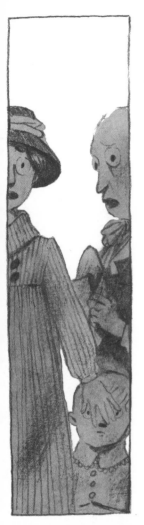

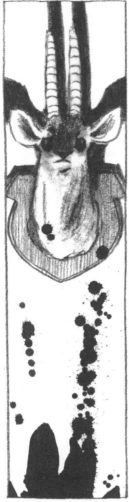

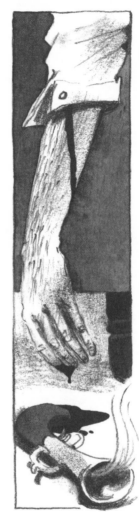

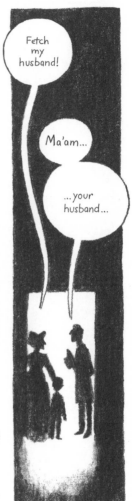

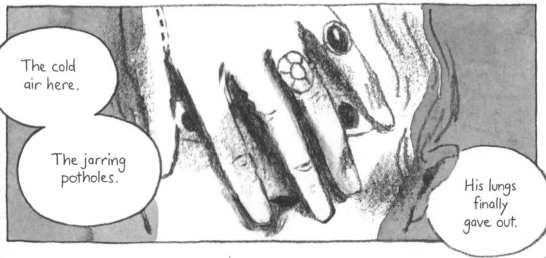

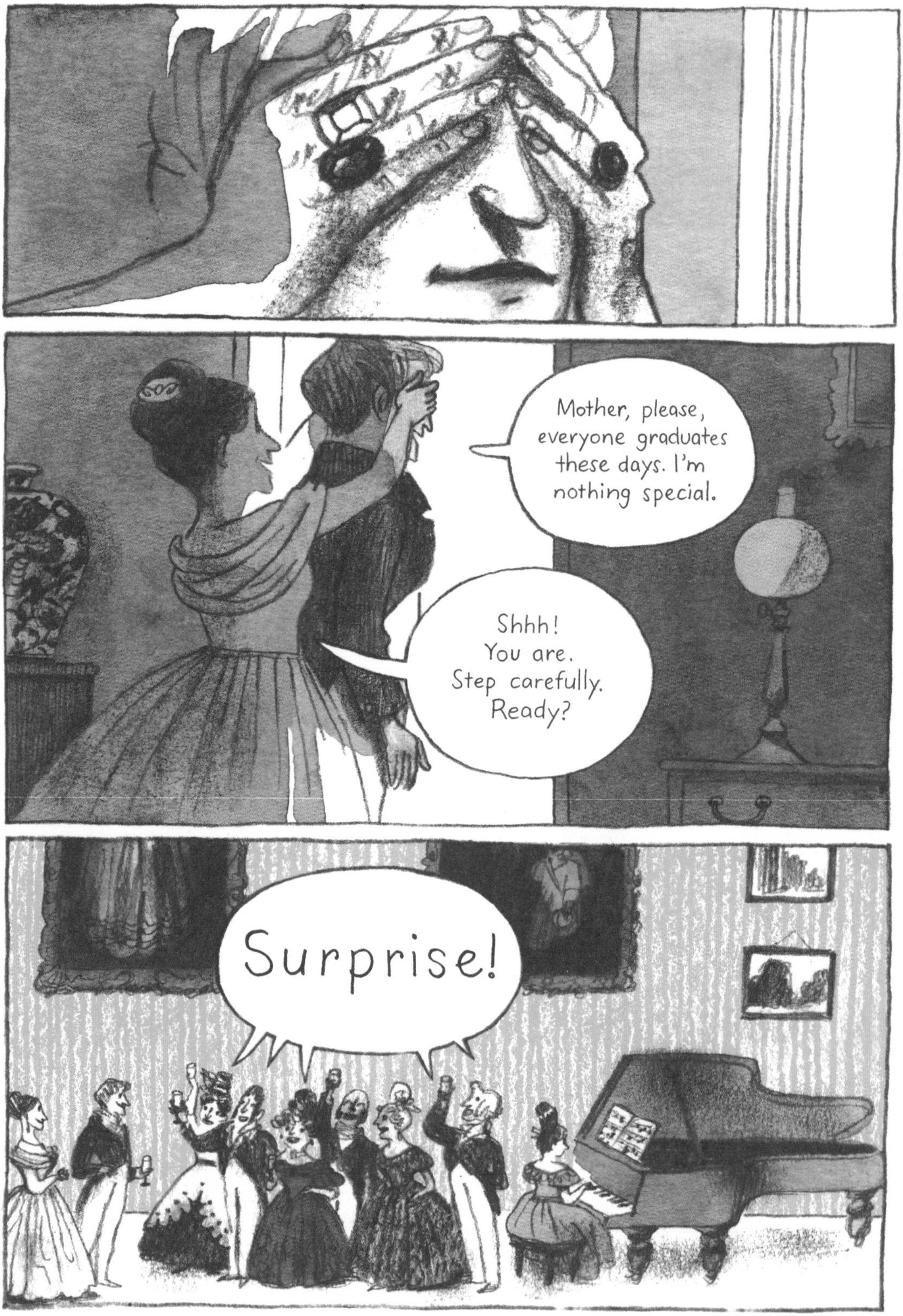
Mother, please, everyone graduates these days. I'm nothing special.
Shhh! You are. Step carefully. Ready?
Surprise!

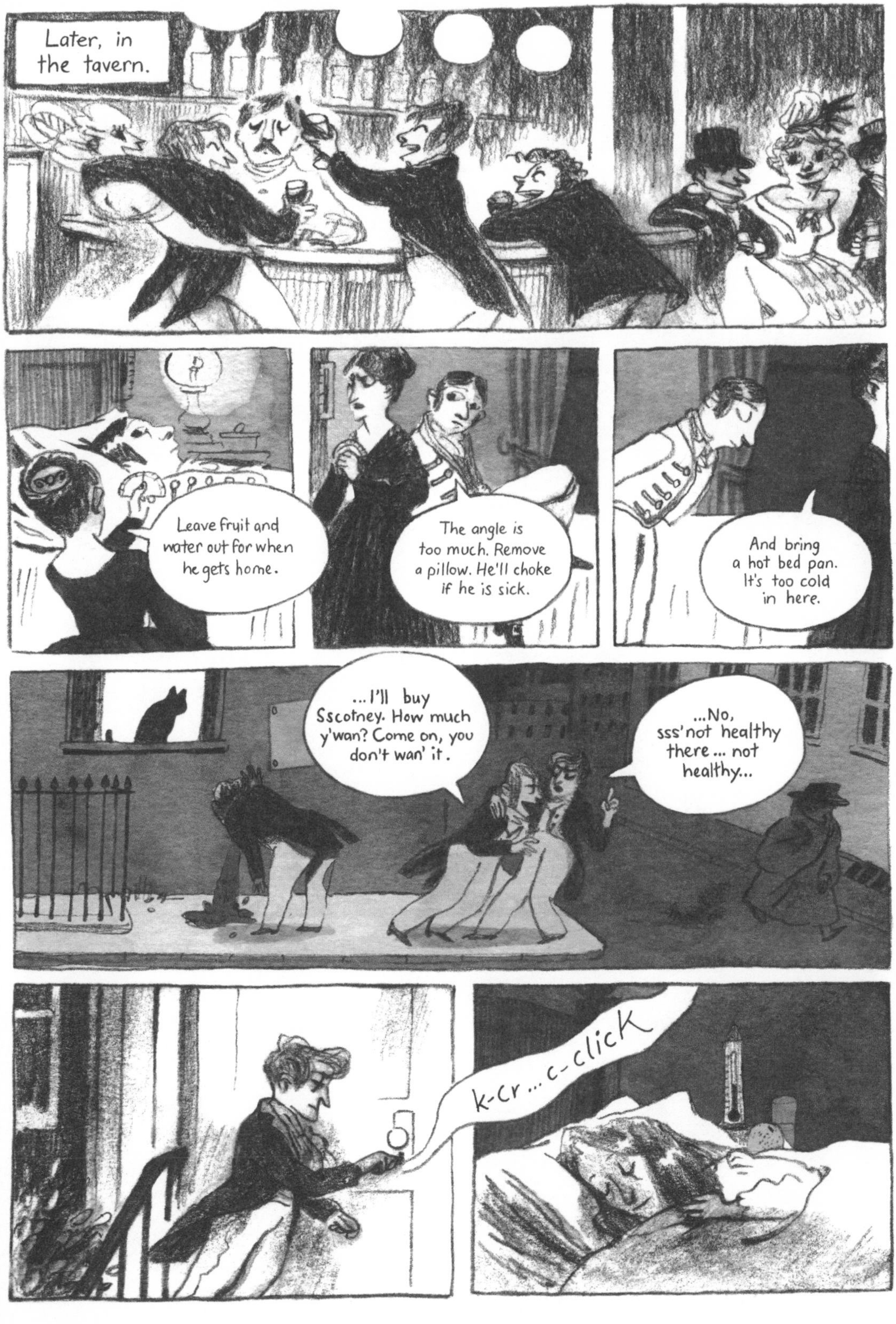
Later, in the tavern.
Leave fruit and water out for when he gets home.
The angle is too much. Remove a pillow. He'll choke if he is sick.
And bring a hot bed pan. It's too cold in here.
...I'll buy Sscotney. How much y'wan? Come on, you don't wan' it.
...No, sss'not healthy there... not healthy...
k-cr... c-click

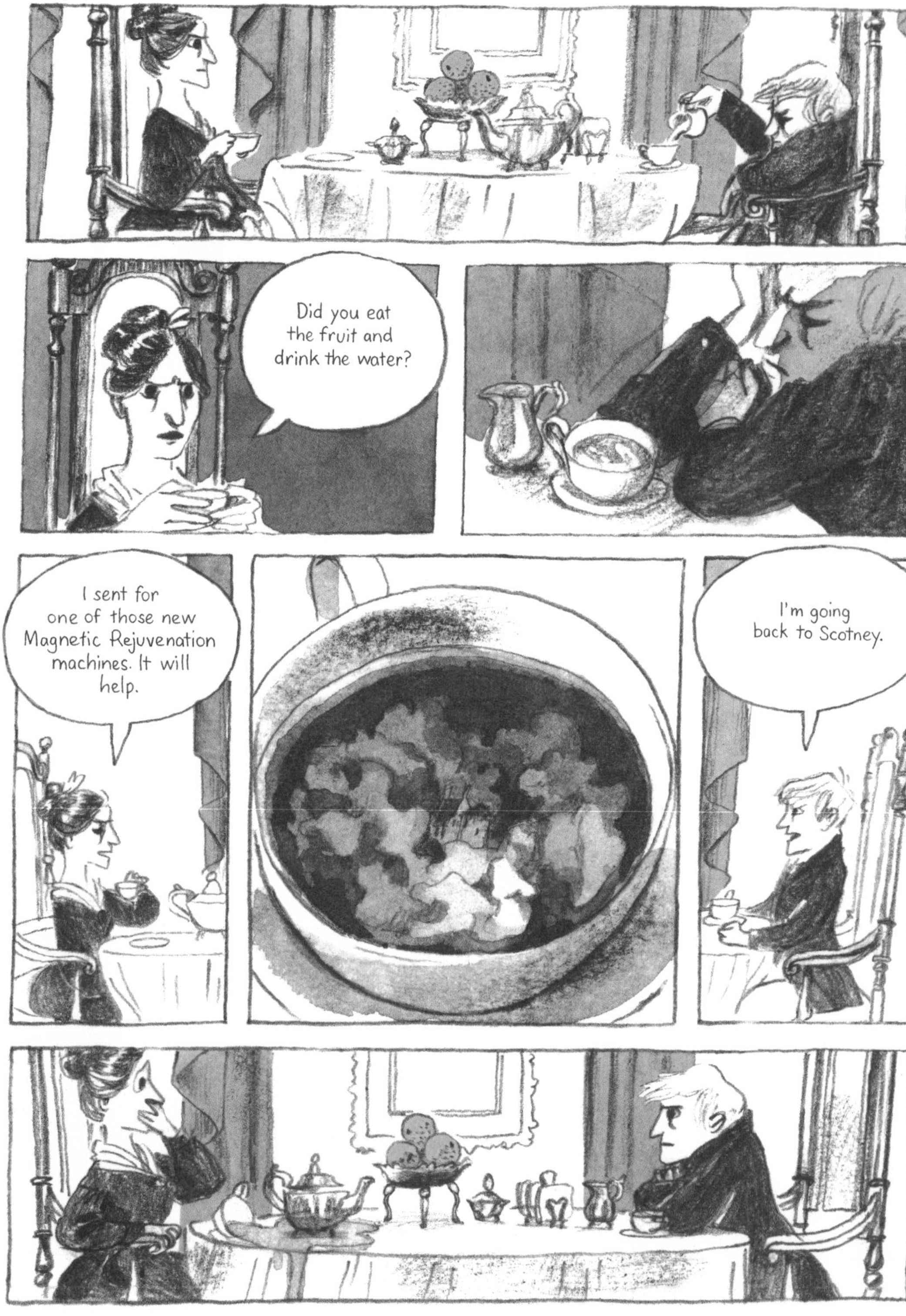
Did you eat the fruit and drink the water?
I sent for one of those new Magnetic Rejuvenation machines. It will help.
I'm going back to Scotney.

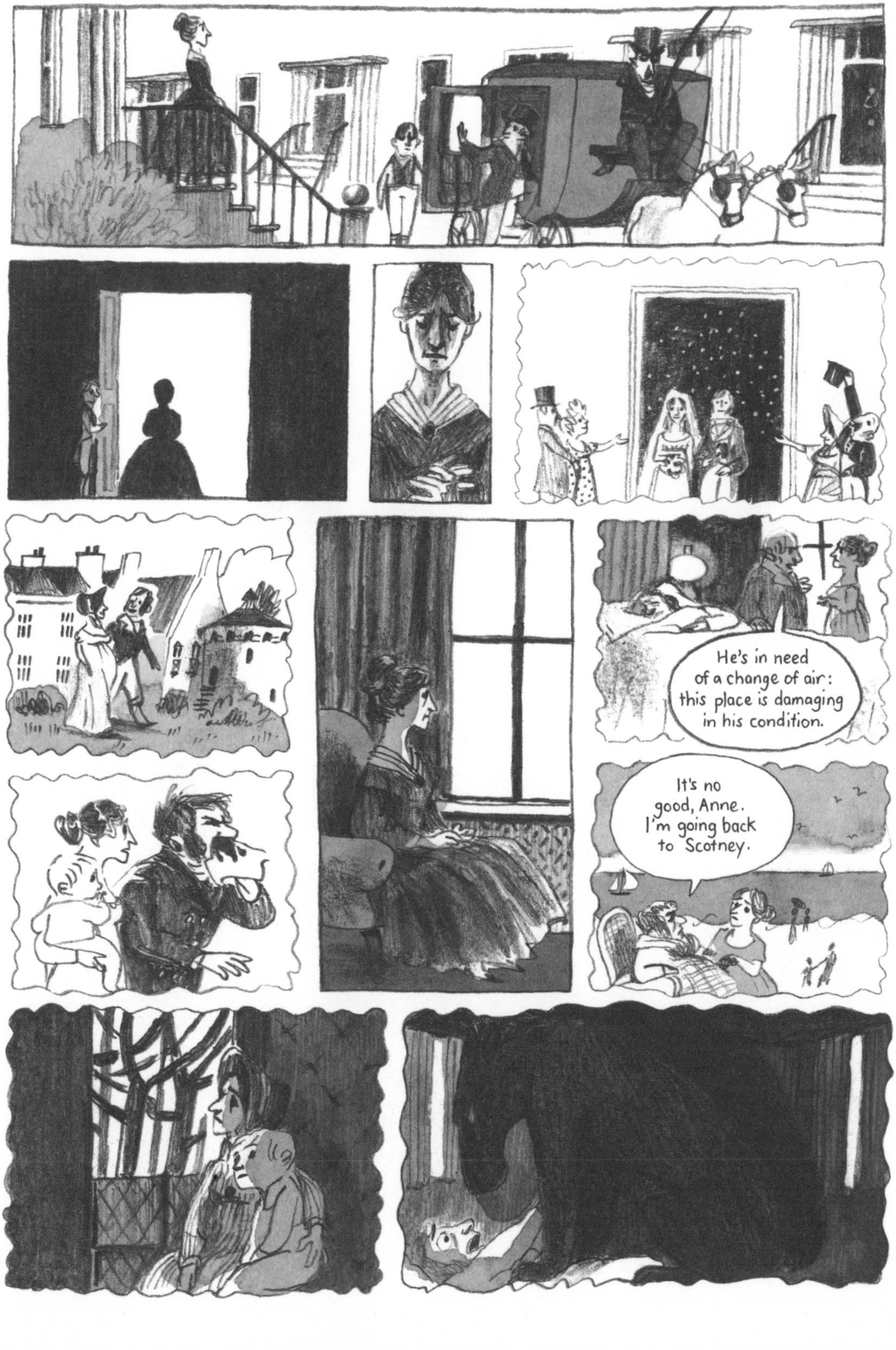
He's in need of a change of air: this place is damaging in his condition.
It's no good, Anne. I'm going back to Scotney.

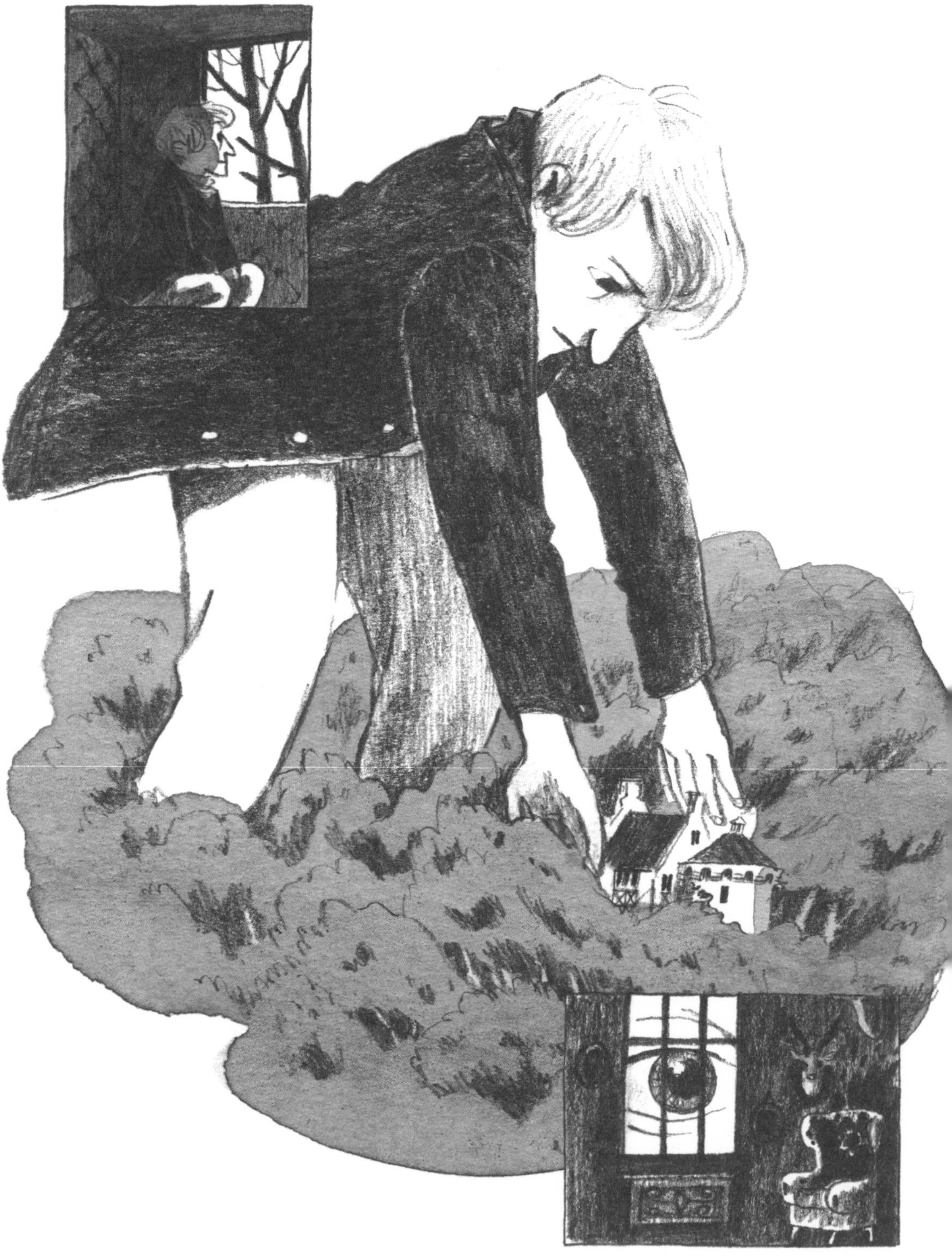

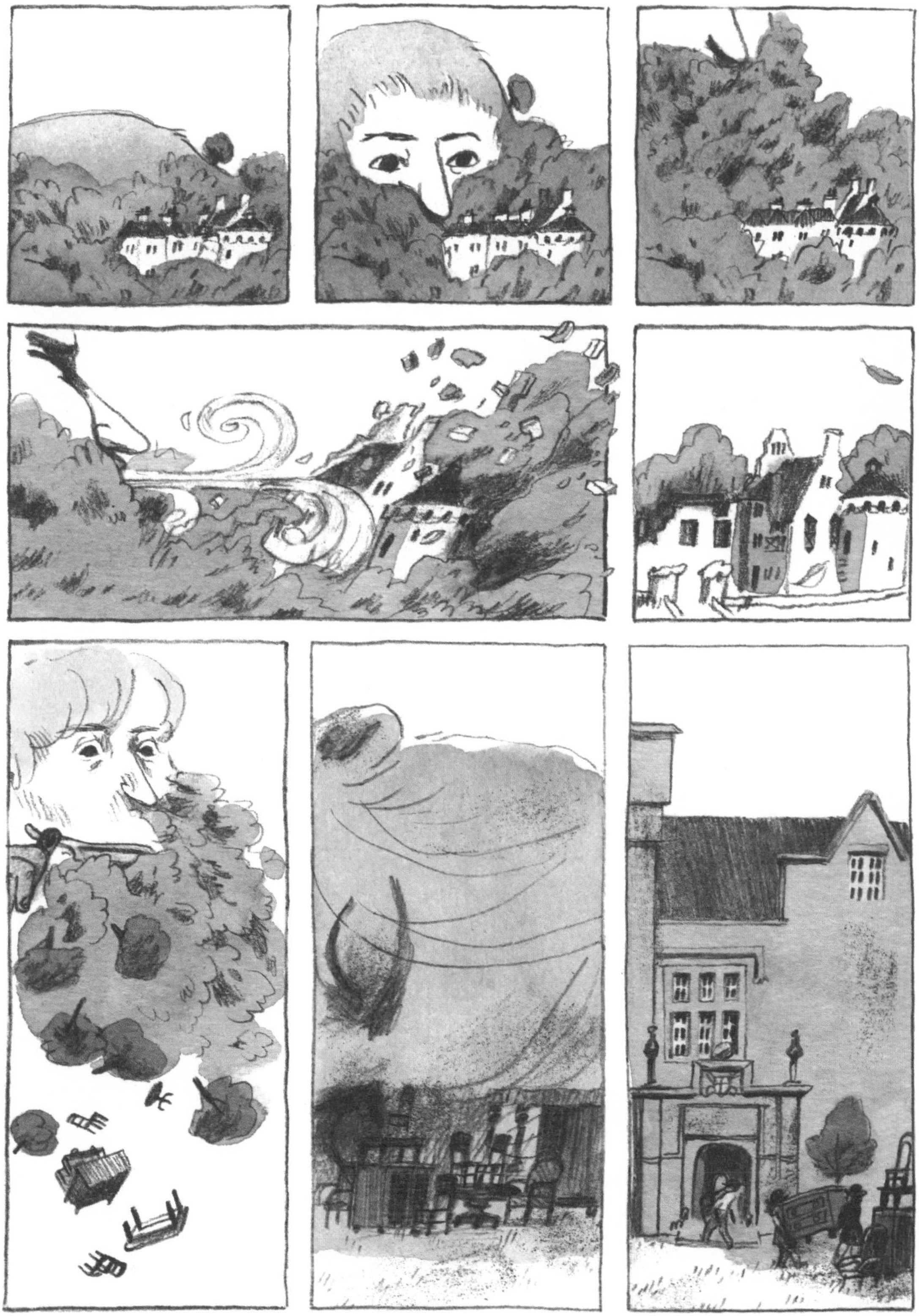

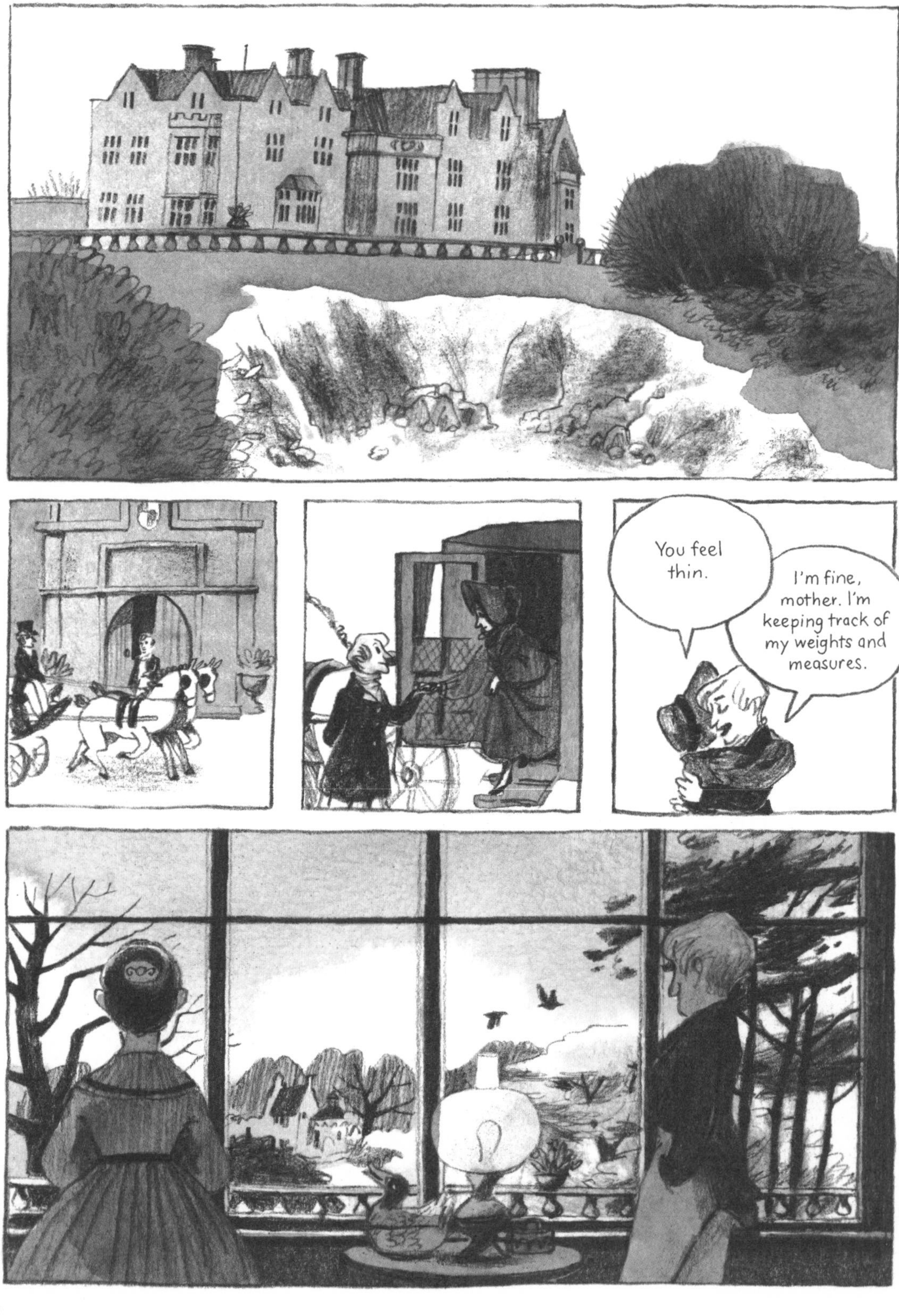
You feel thin.
I'm fine, mother. I'm keeping track of my weights and measures.

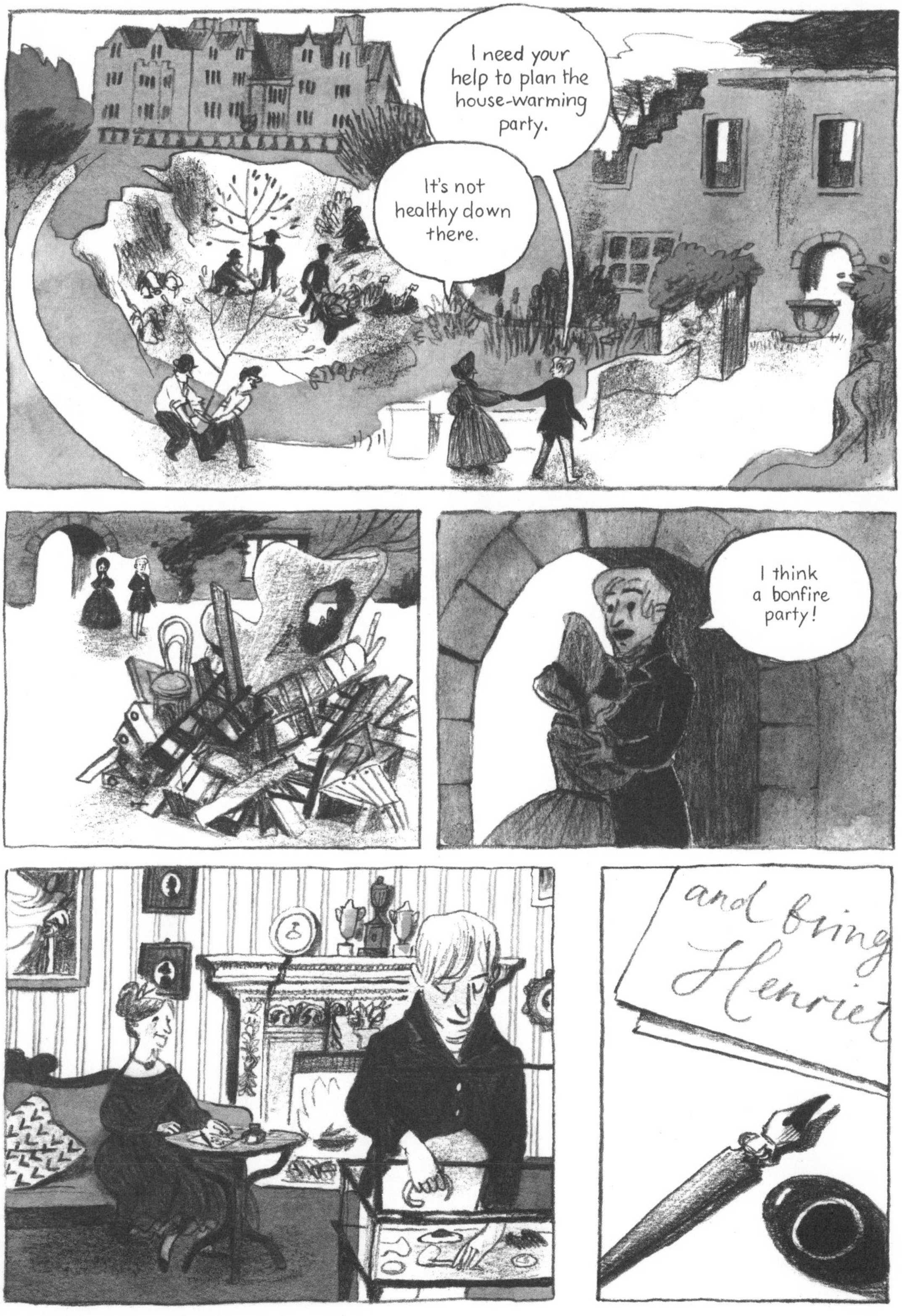
I need your help to plan the house-warming party.
It's not healthy down there.
I think a bonfire party!
and bring Henriet

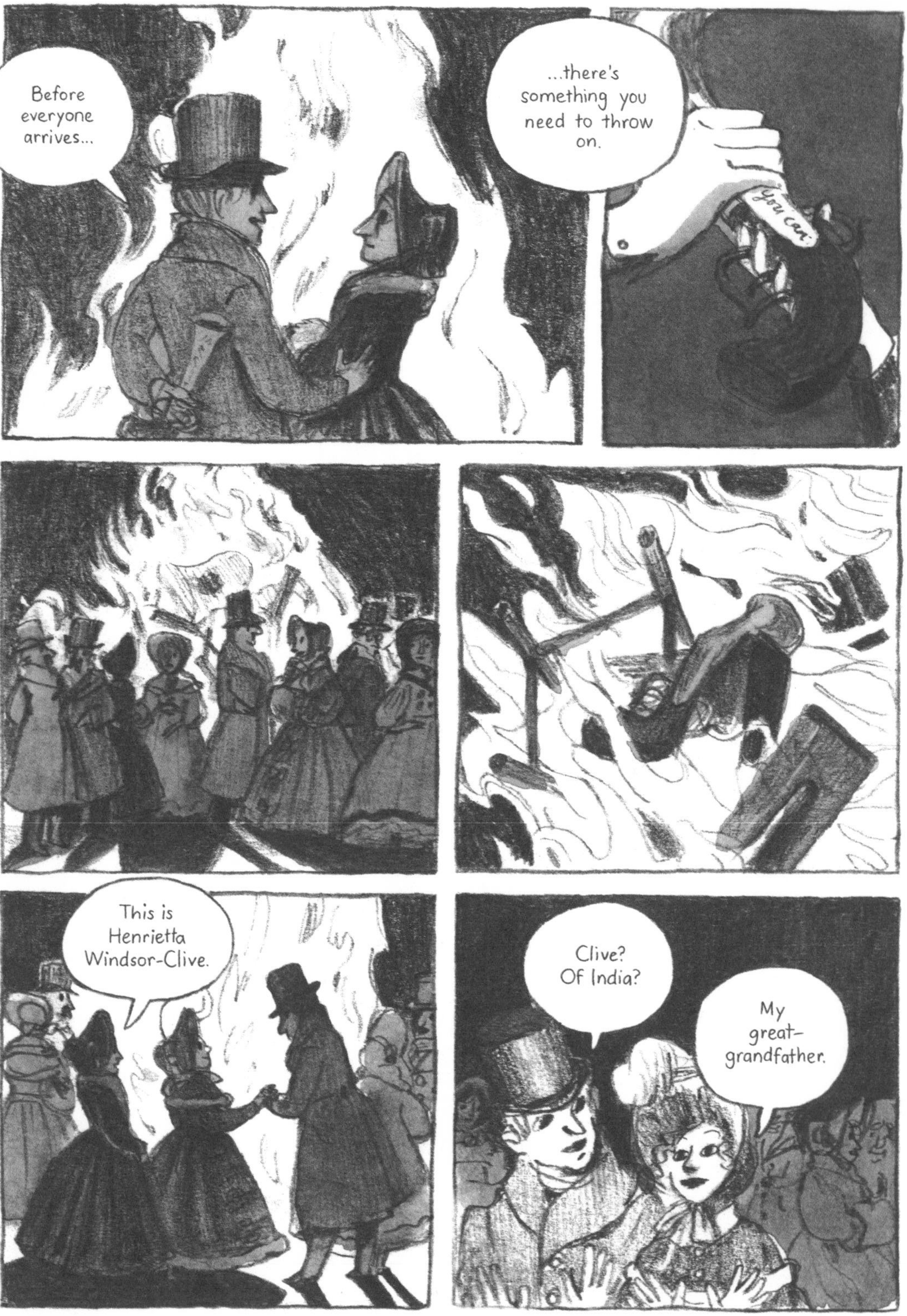
Before everyone arrives...
...there's something you need to throw on.
You can
This is Henrietta Windsor-Clive.
Clive? Of India?
My great-grandfather.

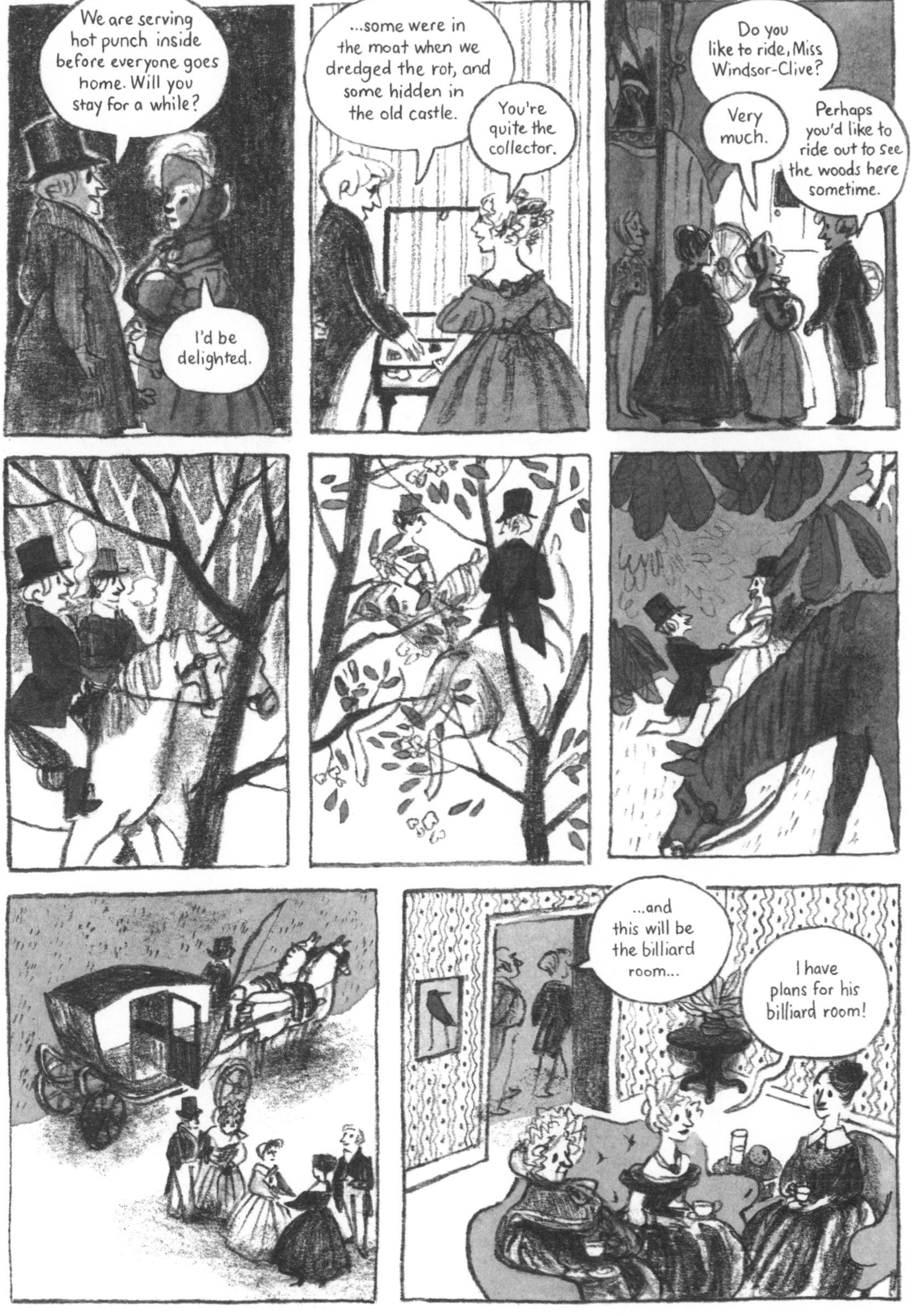
We are serving hot punch inside before everyone goes home. Will you stay for a while?
I'd be delighted.
...some were in the moat when we dredged the rot, and some hidden in the old castle.
You're quite the collector.
Do you like to ride, Miss Windsor-Clive?
Very much.
Perhaps you'd like to ride out to see the woods here sometime.
...and this will be the billiard room...
I have plans for his billiard room!

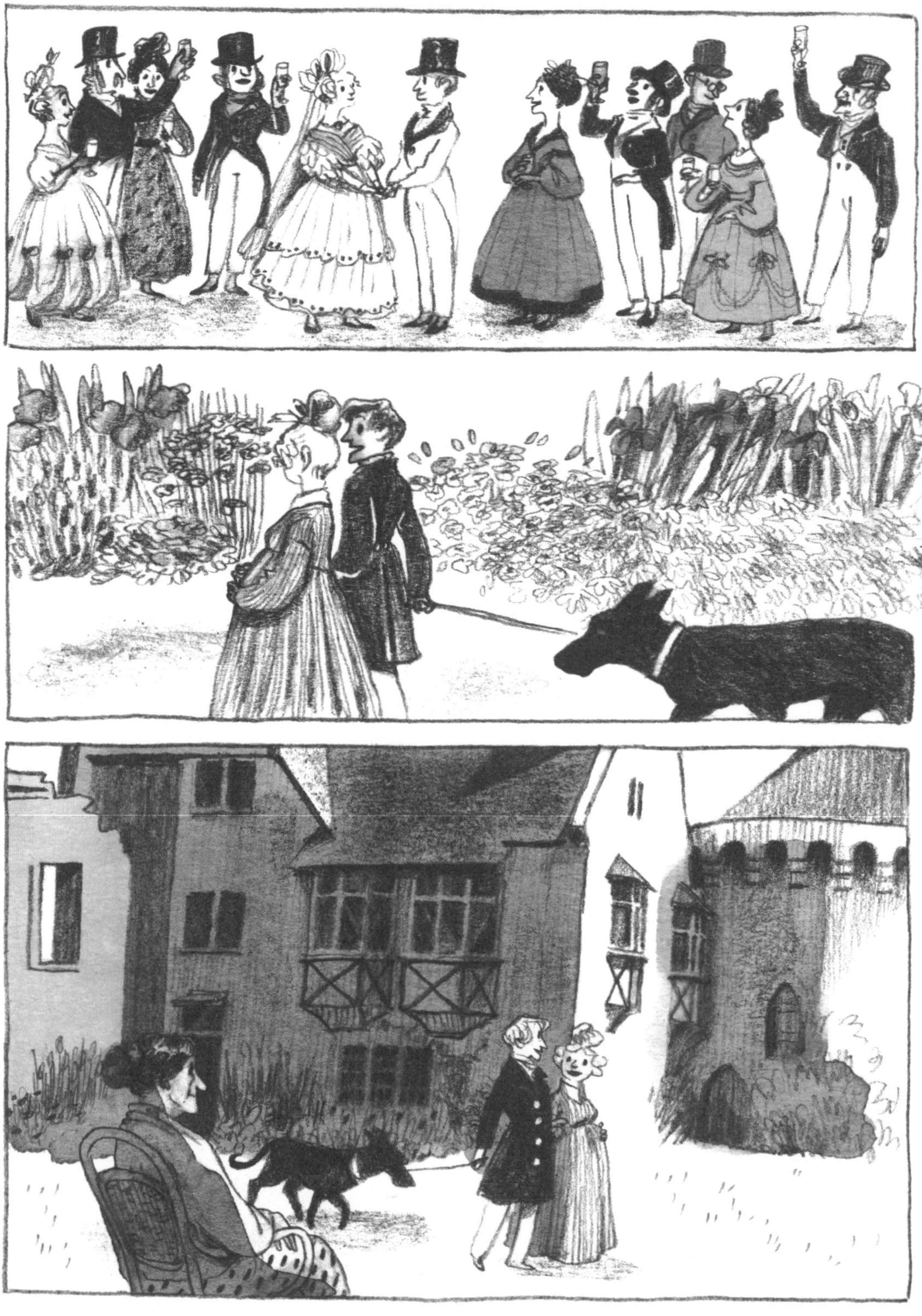

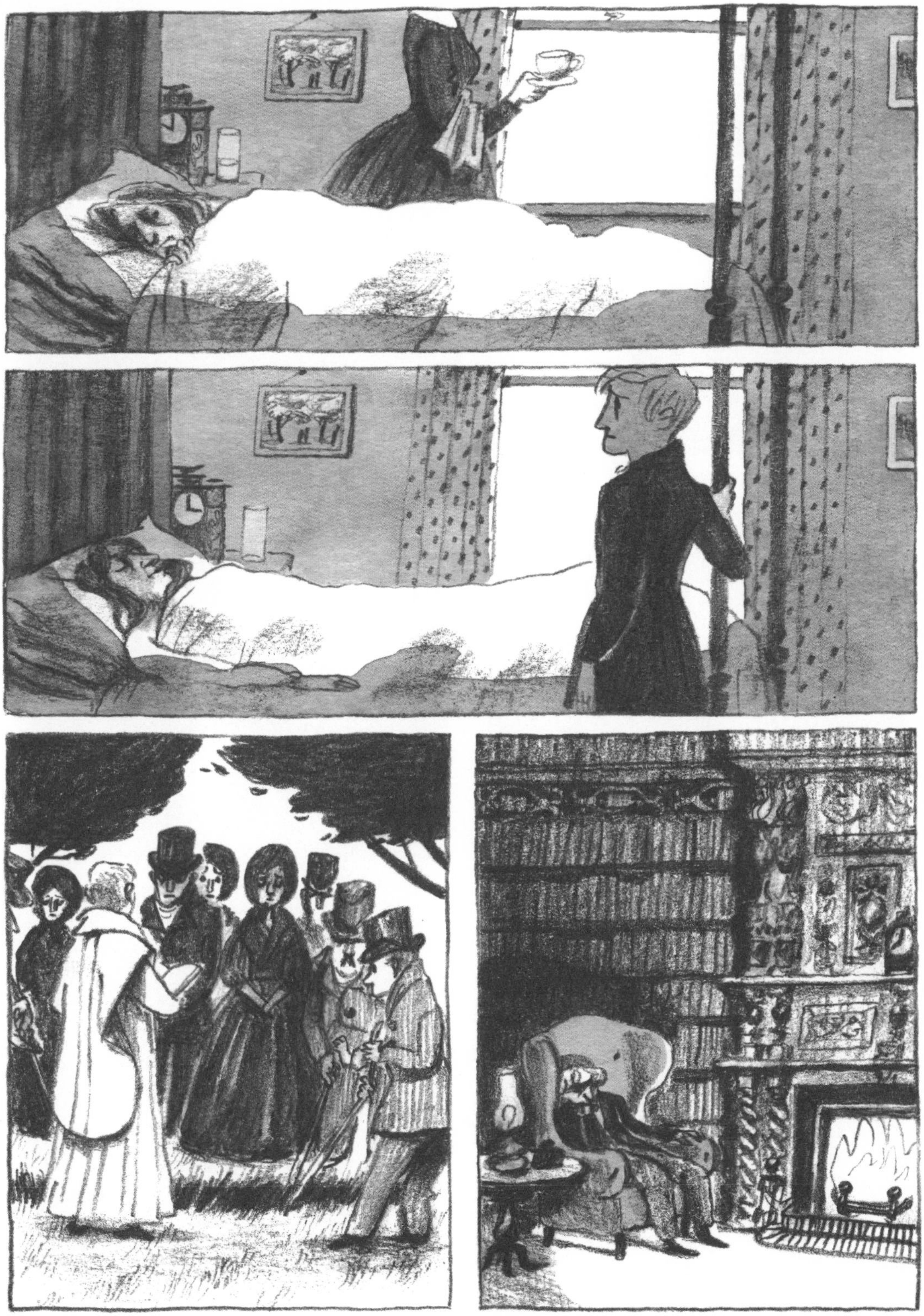

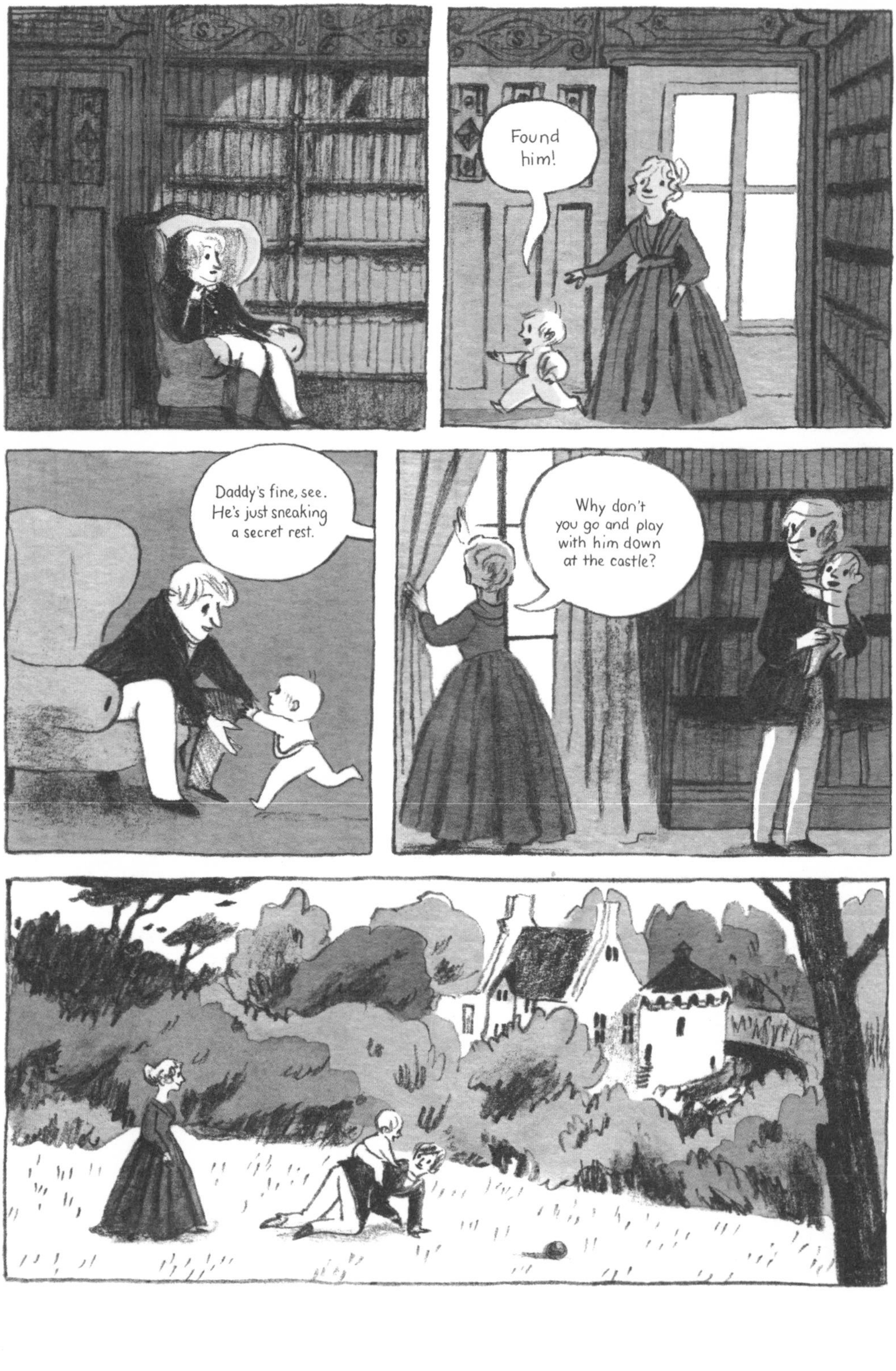

Found him!
Daddy's fine, see. He's just sneaking a secret rest.
Why don't you go and play with him down at the castle?

THE WIDOW
Historical Context

1. After the battle of Waterloo in 1815 came a long period of peace and prosperity during which those who could afford not to work were able to divert their attentions to the study of the sciences and arts.

2. Scientific advances meant that wealthy people were becoming more interested in, and able to influence, their health. Sanitation reforms were made and soap was the main product shown in the relatively new phenomenon of advertising. Aristocrats wanted to be seen to have the best and newest technologies on the market, which drove the rise of an increasingly bizarre and elaborate array of inventions. Several such inventions feature in the Scotney Castle collection.

3. This period saw "The Great Exhibition" – the first World's Fair, which showcased the greatest innovations of the century. The emergence of photography, showcased at the Great Exhibition, resulted in significant changes in Victorian art, with Queen Victoria being the first British monarch to be photographed.

4. Gothic revival architecture was in vogue with the upper classes, and the picturesque movement was beginning to flourish. As part of this style, the old castle at Scotney was deliberately ruined to create a dramatic folly ruin as part of the landscape on wealthy estates.

Factual Background at Scotney Castle

1. In 1816 the owner of Scotney Castle, Edward Hussey I, in the depths of depression, committed suicide with a blunderbuss. One year later, Edward Hussey II died of a long-term illness, leaving his widow, Anne, and young son Edward Hussey III (then 10 years old). Anne took Edward III away, believing the old castle to be a deeply unhealthy place and responsible for her father-in-law's suicide and husband's illness.

2. When Edward returned to the castle as an adult, he deliberately ruined the castle to make it a feature of the picturesque landscape, using some of the stone, along with stone quarried from part of the castle estate, to build a new manor house on a nearby hill. The manor house was built with a meticulous attention to detail; Edward had 33 meetings with architect Anthony Salvin whilst planning the new house.

3. Edward and his mother, Anne, lived together in the new manor house alone for 13 years until Edward finally married Henrietta Windsor-Clive. Henrietta then moved into the house, and she and Edward had six children.

4. The castle collection contains diaries and letters detailing Anne and Edward's interest in health (something I feel must stem from their traumatic experience in Edward's childhood). The family kept a log of external temperatures as well as a 'weights' book for themselves and their guests. Edward also makes many references to his health in his 'Memoranda of Important Events' book.

5. In the castle collection there are many Victorian era objects related to health. For example; thermometers in some rooms, a home electric shock therapy kit (in 1800s believed to rejuvenate the body), and an elaborate polished brass enema kit.

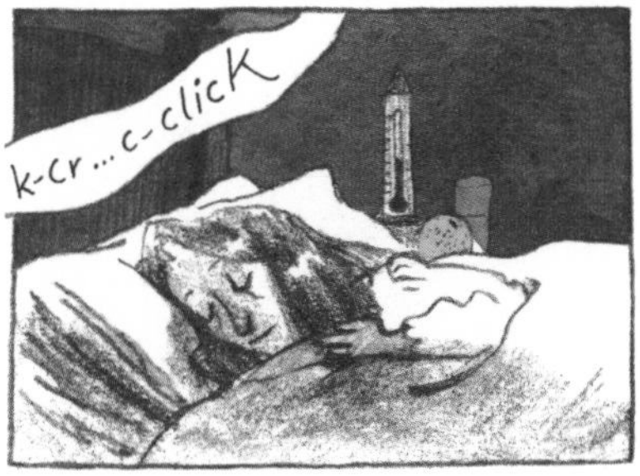
k-cr ... c-click

HUSSEY FAMILY TREE

From the Victorian Era onwards

Edward Windsor Hussey
(1855 - 1952)

William Clive Hussey
(1858 - 1929)

Gertrude Anne Hussey
(1861 - 1921)

Married
Mary-Anne Herbert Daughter of the
Very Rev. Hon. George Herbert,
Dean of Hereford
(1898)

Christopher Edward
Clive Hussey
(1899 - 1970)

Barbara Winifred
(1904 - 1987)

Married
Elizabeth-Maud Kerr-Smiley
(1936)

Married
Timothy Charles Adison Bidey
(1943)

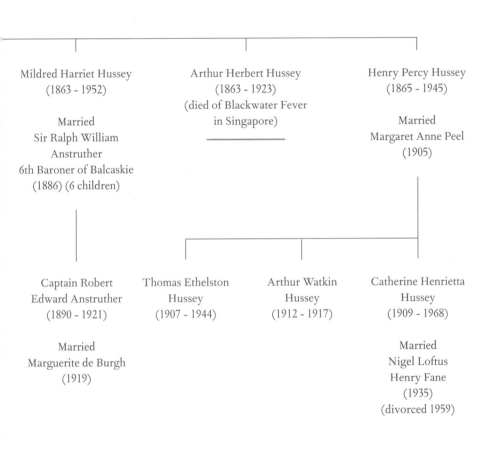

Mildred Harriet Hussey
(1863 - 1952)

Married
Sir Ralph William
Anstruther
6th Baroner of Balcaskie
(1886) (6 children)

Arthur Herbert Hussey
(1863 - 1923)
(died of Blackwater Fever
in Singapore)
——————————

Henry Percy Hussey
(1865 - 1945)

Married
Margaret Anne Peel
(1905)

Captain Robert
Edward Anstruther
(1890 - 1921)

Married
Marguerite de Burgh
(1919)

Thomas Ethelston
Hussey
(1907 - 1944)

Arthur Watkin
Hussey
(1912 - 1917)

Catherine Henrietta
Hussey
(1909 - 1968)

Married
Nigel Loftus
Henry Fane
(1935)
(divorced 1959)

————— Persons marked red feature in the story 'The Hunter'

THE HUNTER

by Isabel Greenberg

Britain is at its most powerful in economic terms,
with the Empire still covering vast swathes of the
world and London being its financial centre. Big
game hunting was a way for wealthy gentlemen to
show what wonderful creatures they had encountered
on their travels. The Hussey family, with four male
children and two female, are living in the new family
mansion overlooking the old castle folly ruin. Arthur
is the third male in line to be heir and so joins the
army, travelling the world and hunting exotic animals.
Nature has a way of fighting back…

Edwardian Era
The age of empire
- 1907 to 1923 -

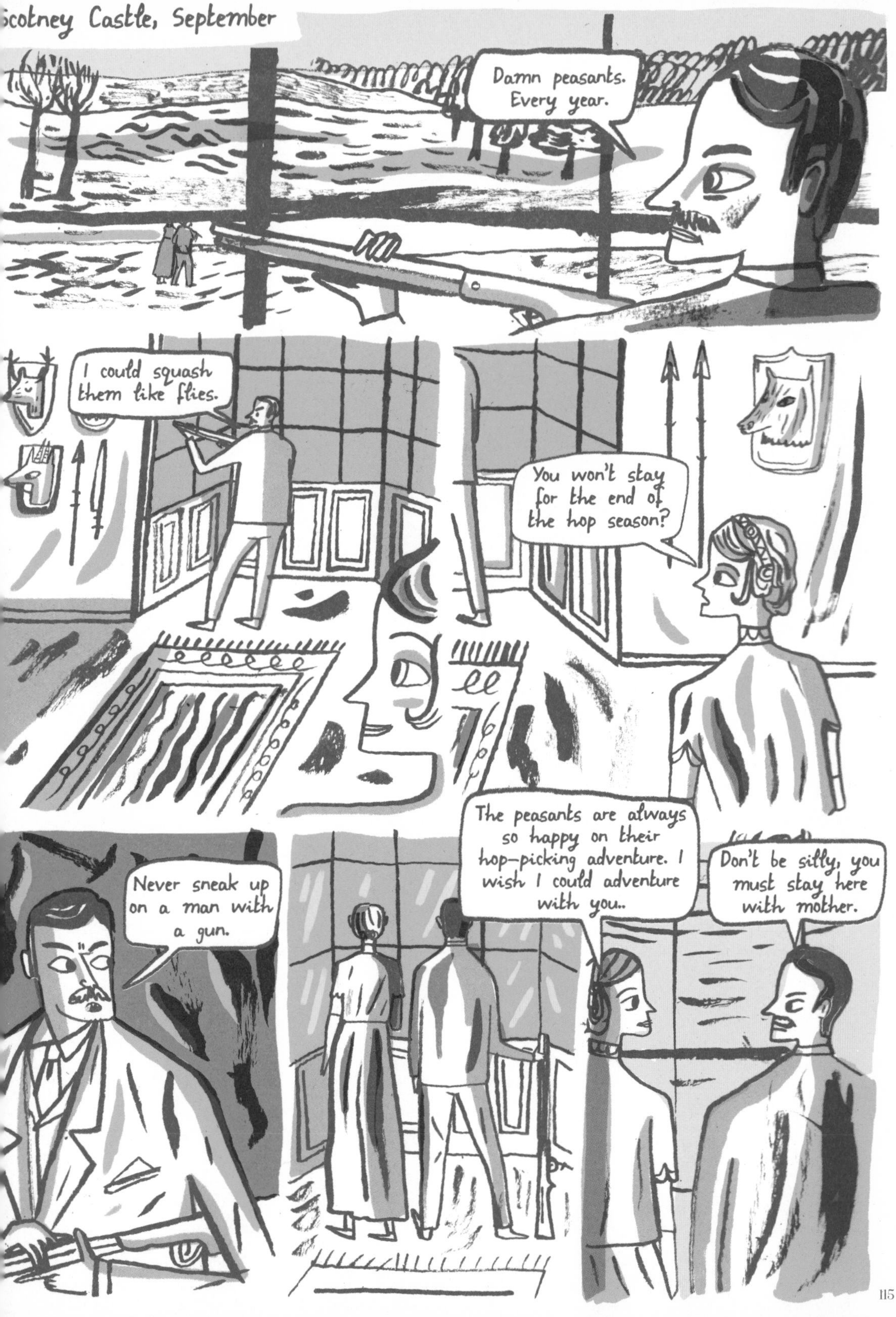
Scotney Castle, September
Damn peasants. Every year.
I could squash them like flies.
You won't stay for the end of the hop season?
Never sneak up on a man with a gun.
The peasants are always so happy on their hop-picking adventure. I wish I could adventure with you..
Don't be silly, you must stay here with mother.

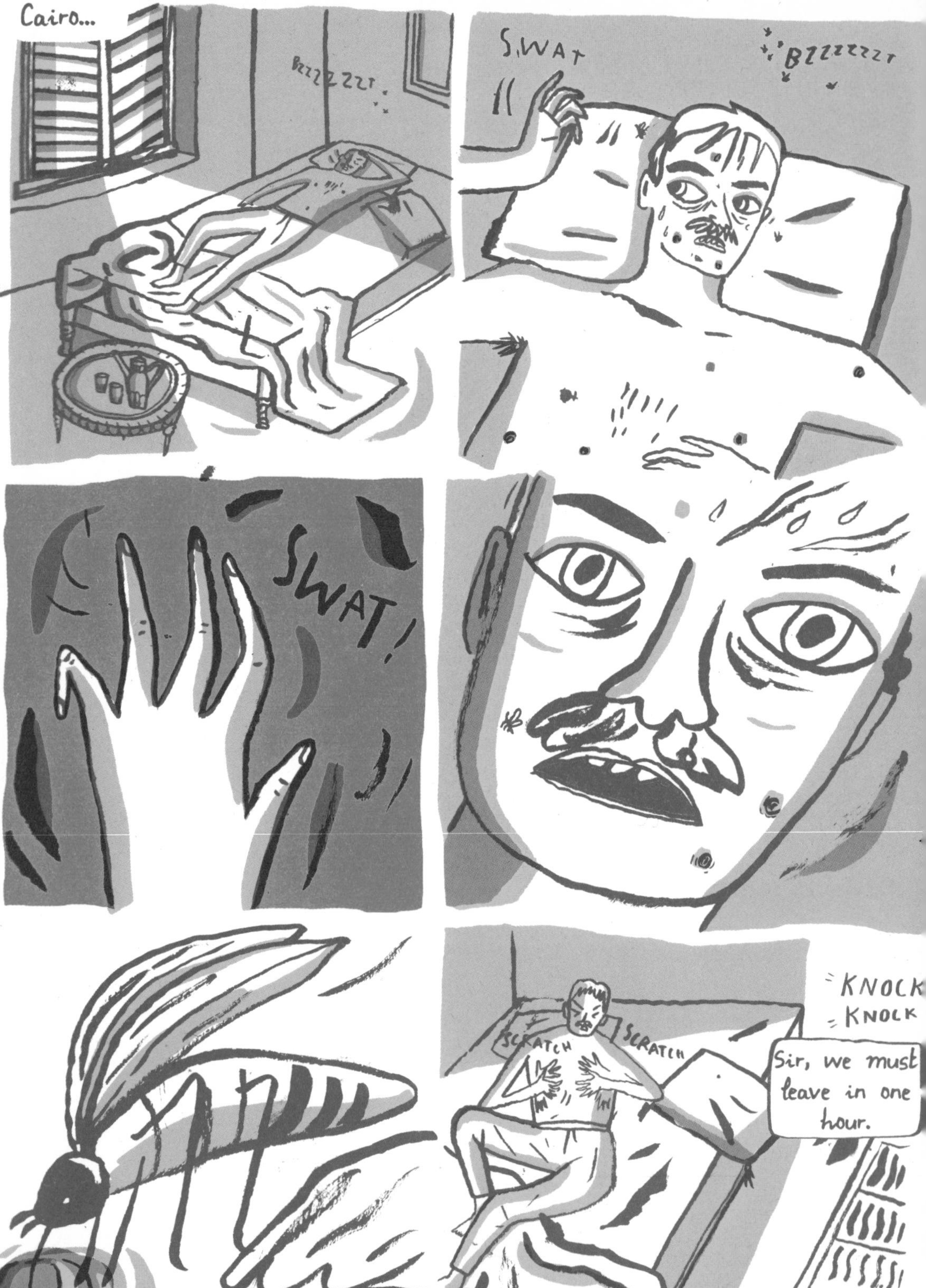
Cairo...
BZZZZZZT
SWAT
BZZZZZZT
SWAT!
SCRATCH
SCRATCH
KNOCK
KNOCK
Sir, we must leave in one hour.

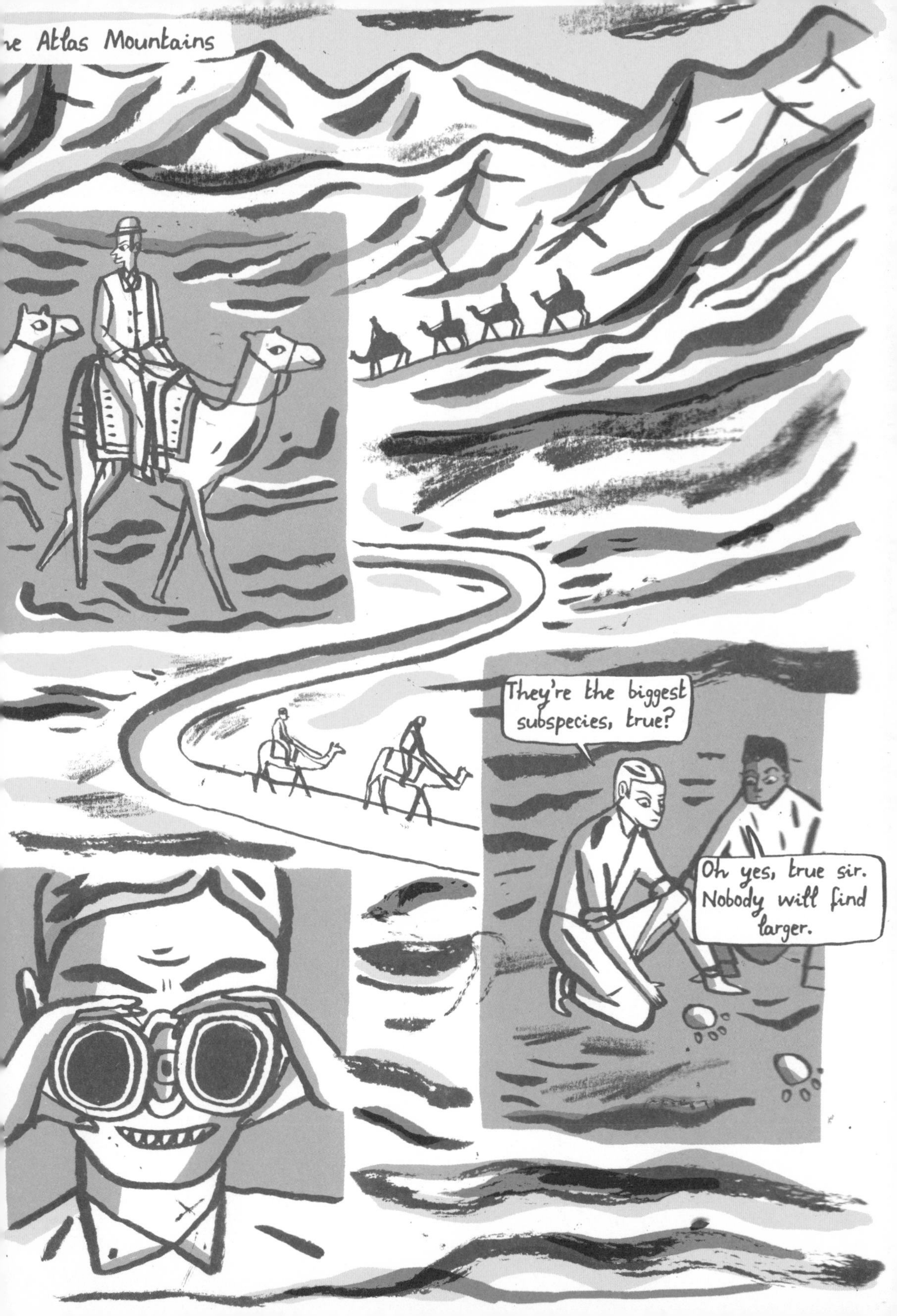
e Atlas Mountains
They're the biggest subspecies, true?
Oh yes, true sir. Nobody will find larger.

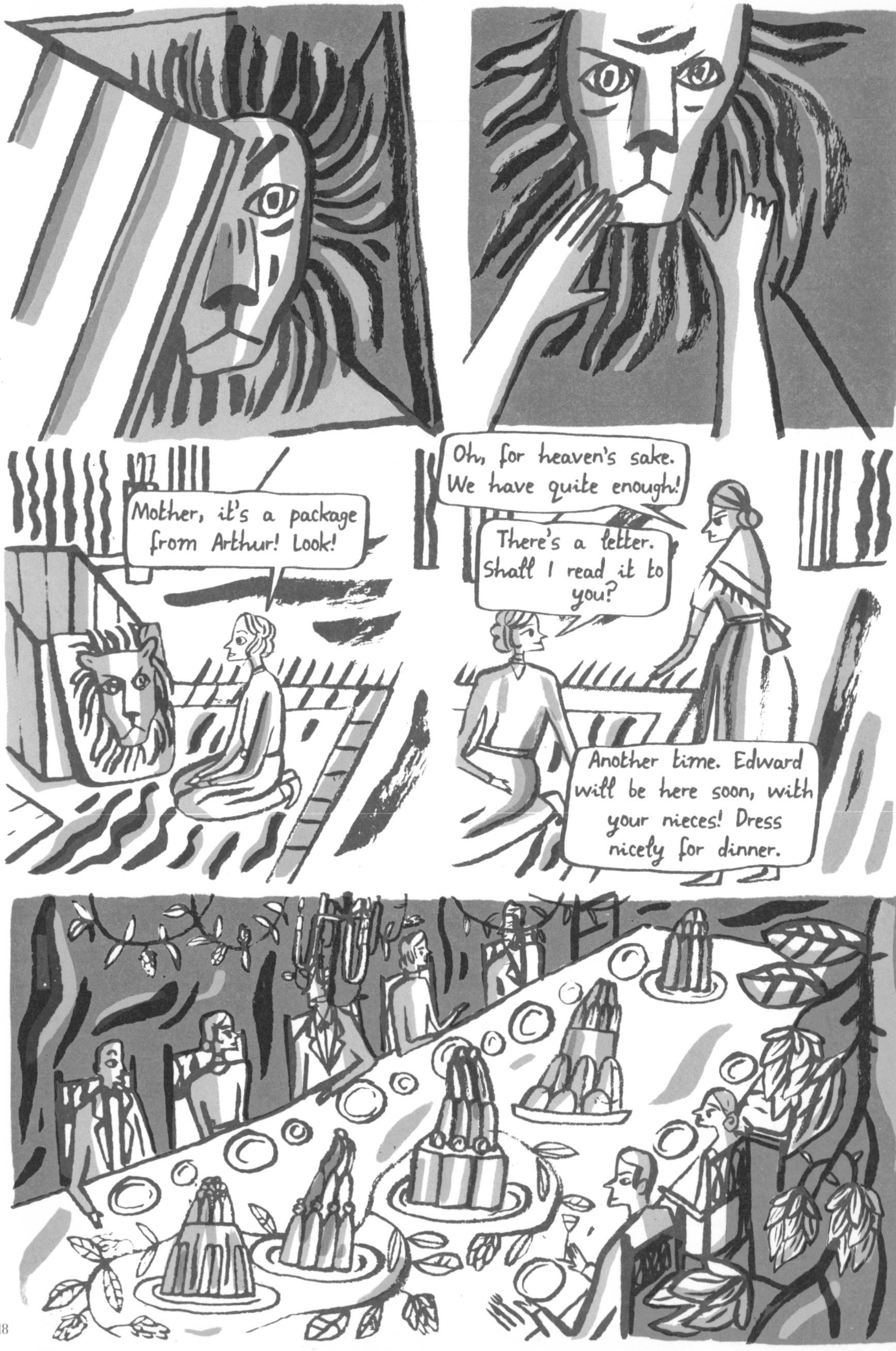
Mother, it's a package from Arthur! Look!
Oh, for heaven's sake. We have quite enough!
There's a letter. Shall I read it to you?
Another time. Edward will be here soon, with your nieces! Dress nicely for dinner.

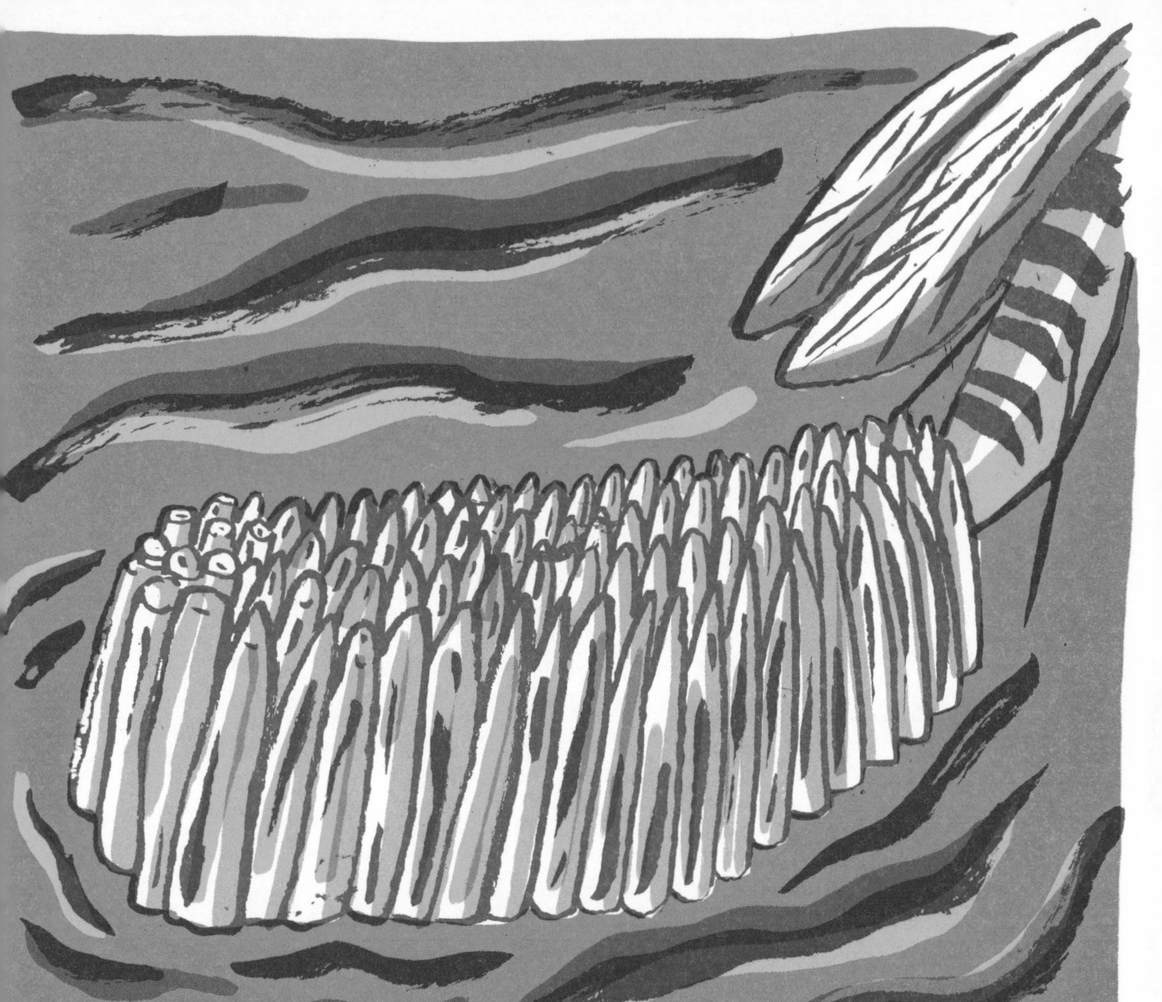

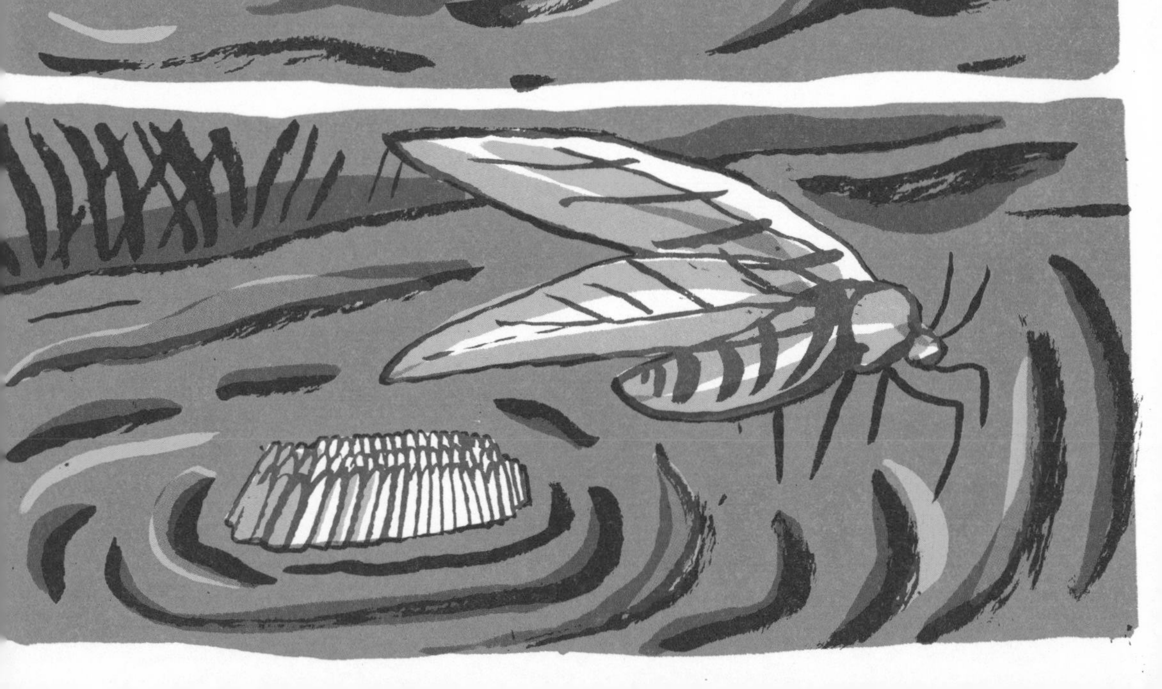

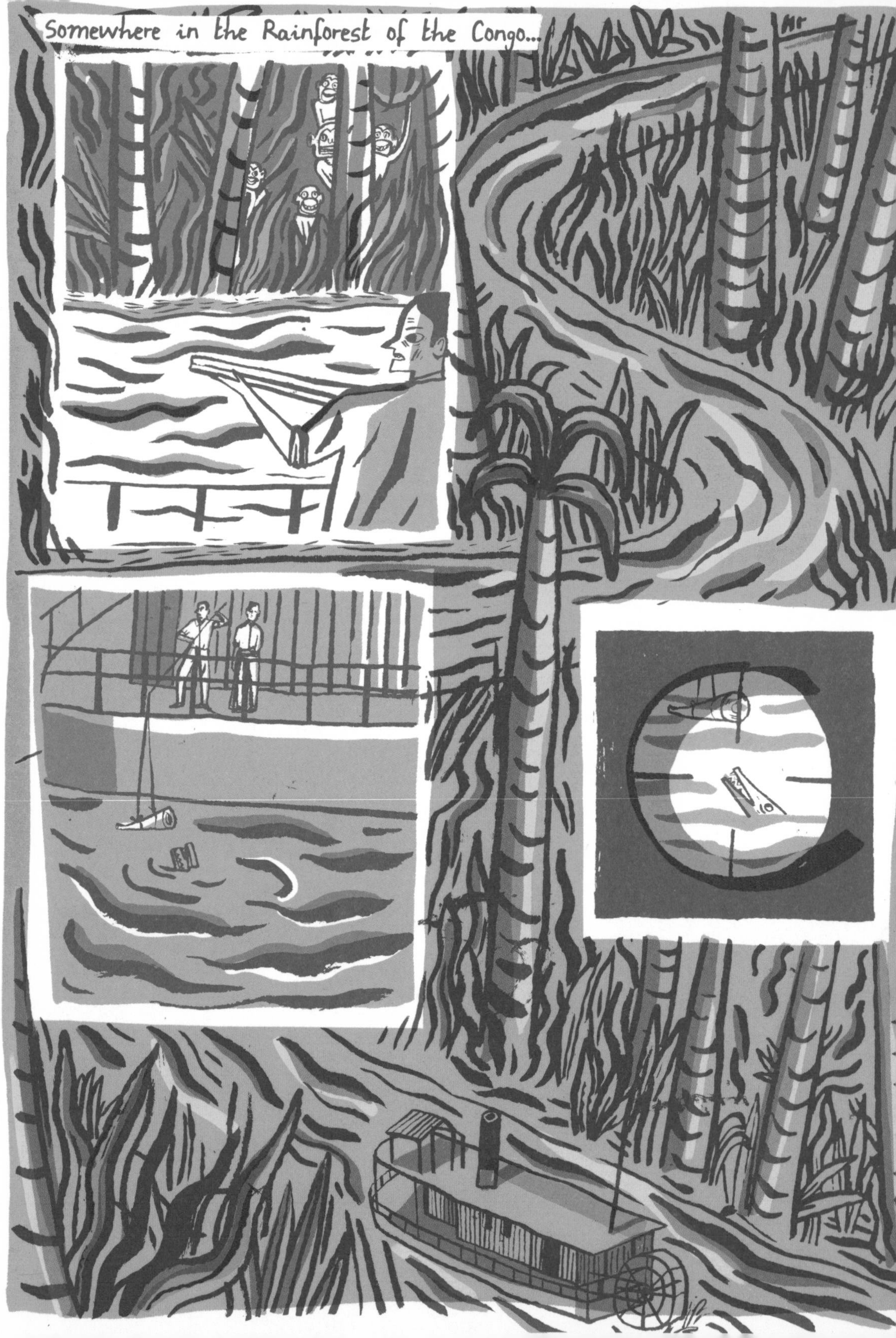
Somewhere in the Rainforest of the Congo...

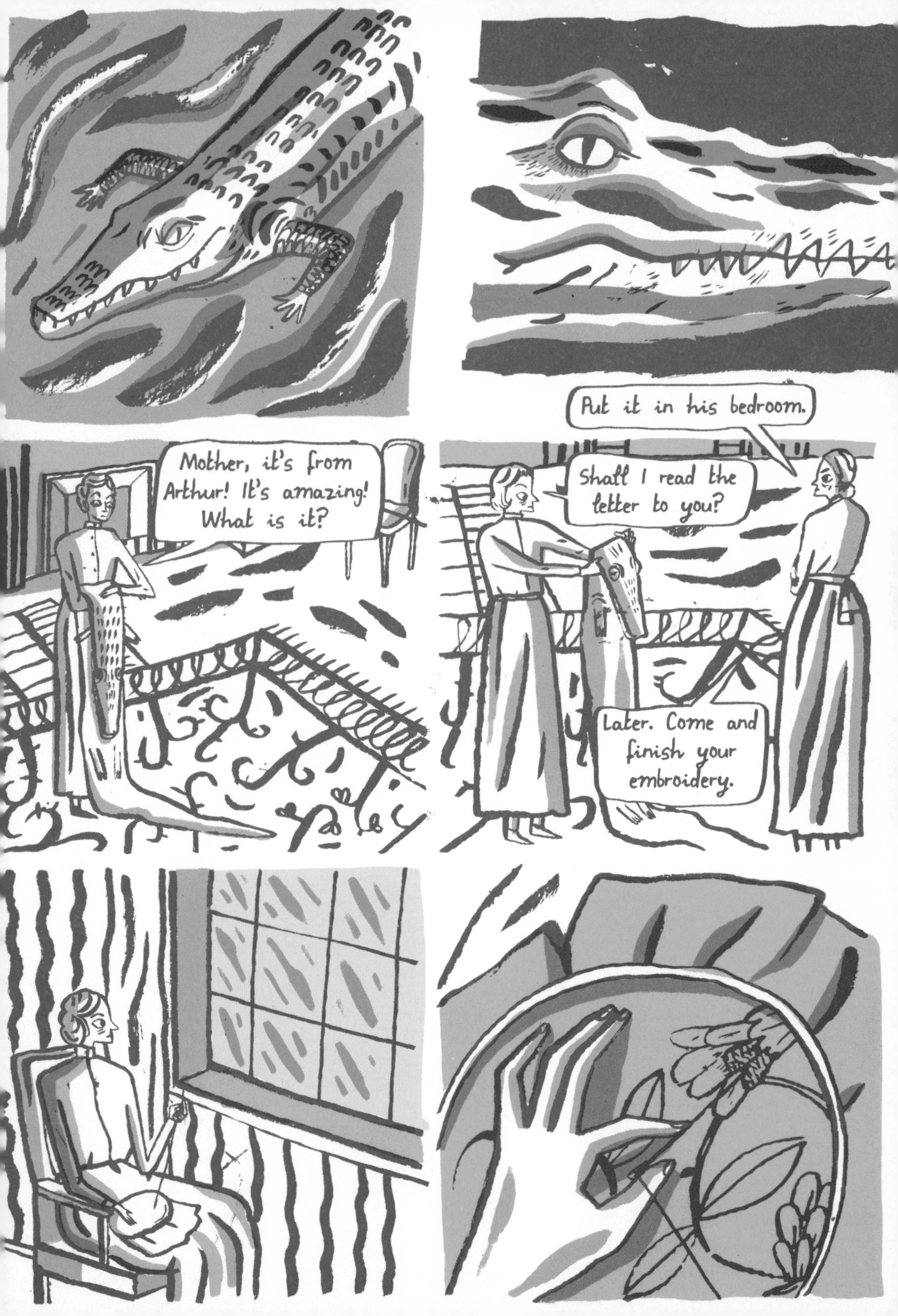
Mother, it's from Arthur! It's amazing! What is it?
Put it in his bedroom.
Shall I read the letter to you?
Later. Come and finish your embroidery.

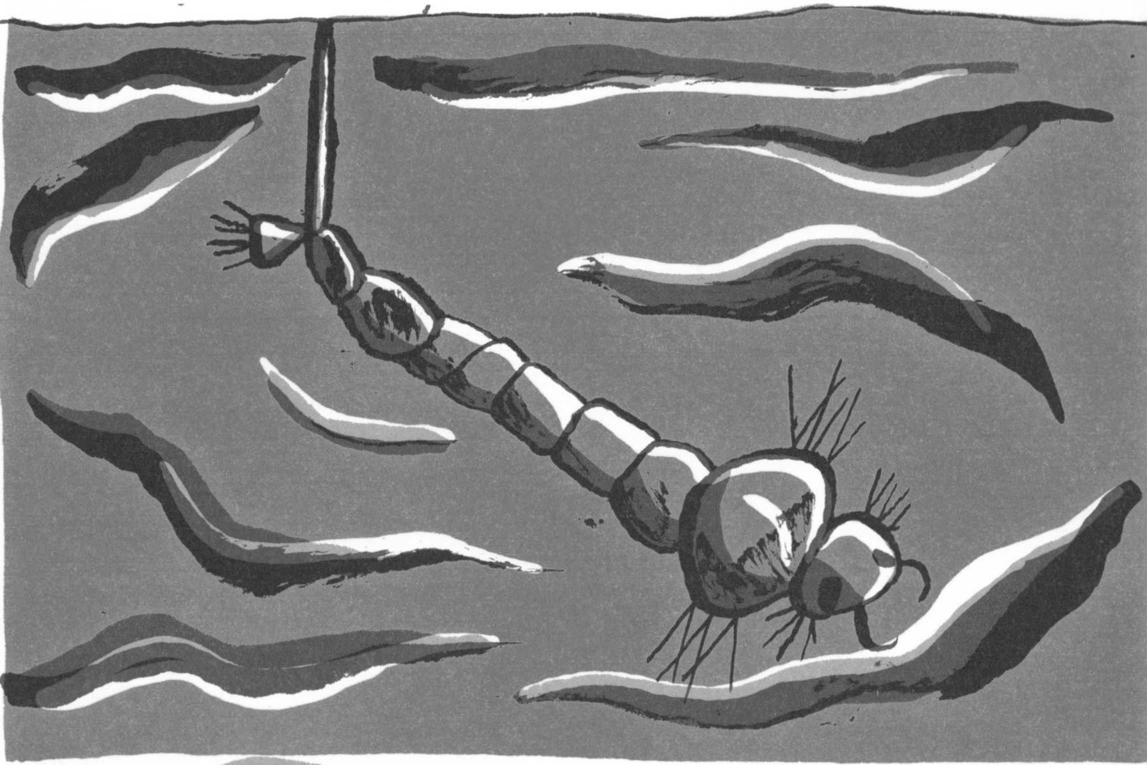

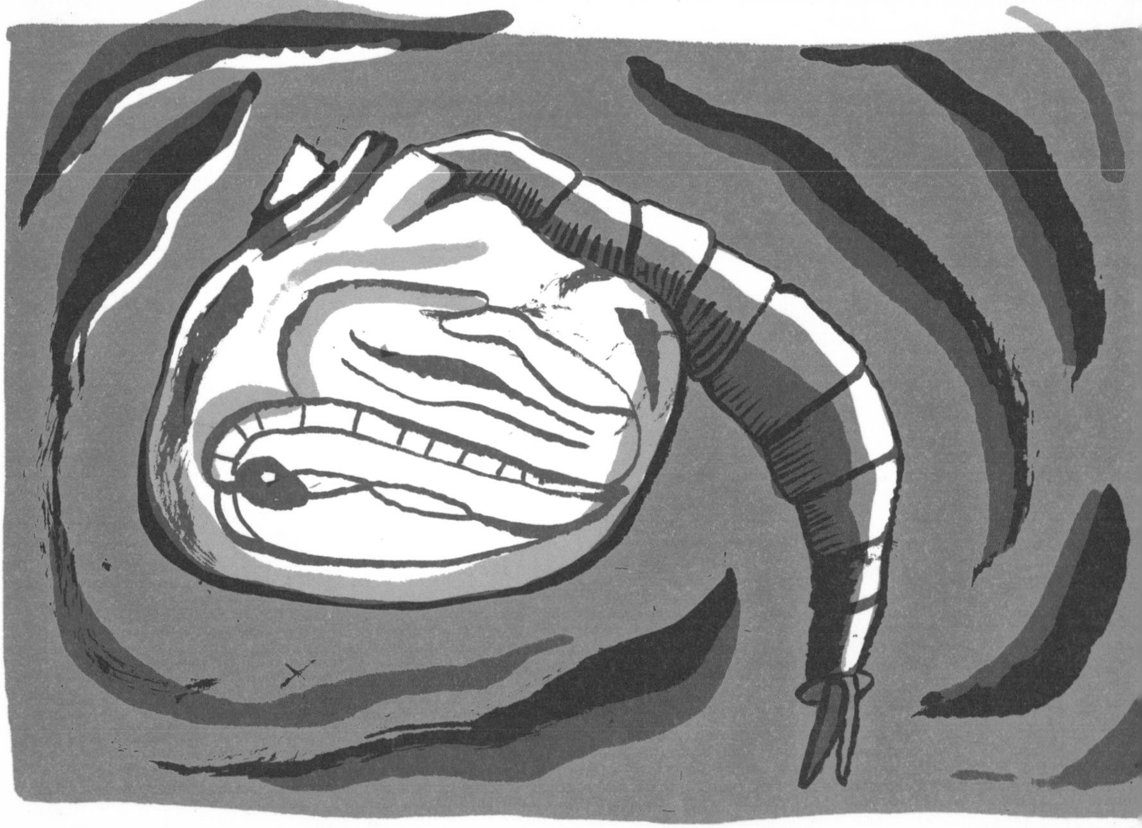

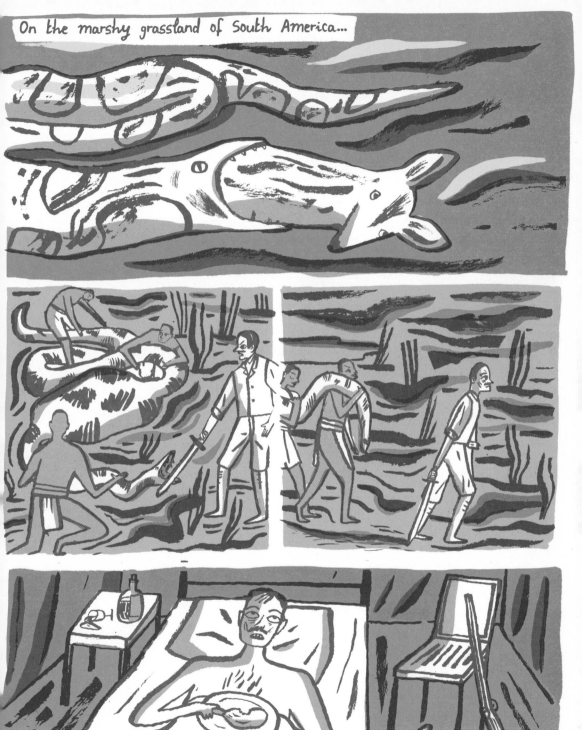

On the marshy grassland of South America...

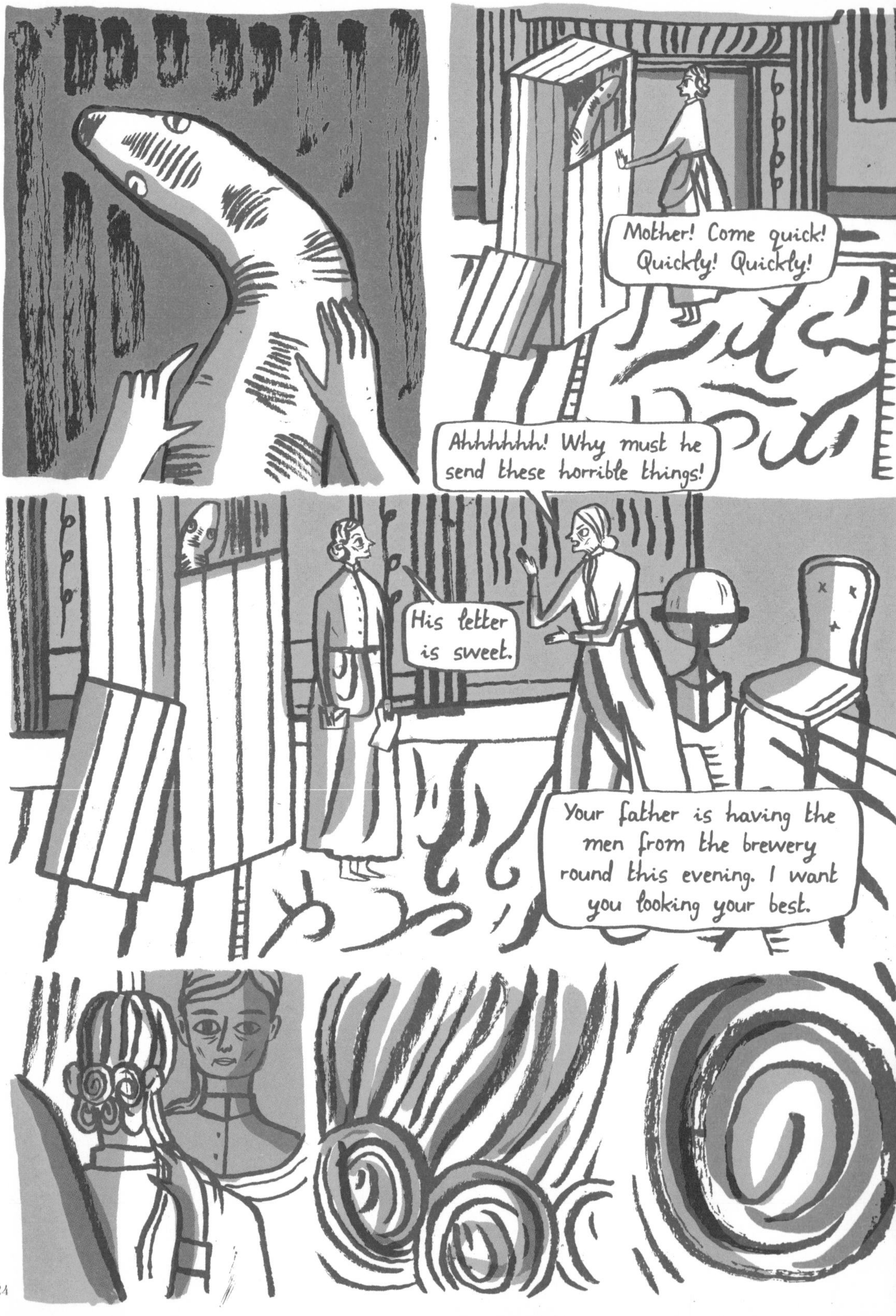
Mother! Come quick! Quickly! Quickly!
Ahhhhhhh! Why must he send these horrible things!
His letter is sweet.
Your father is having the men from the brewery round this evening. I want you looking your best.

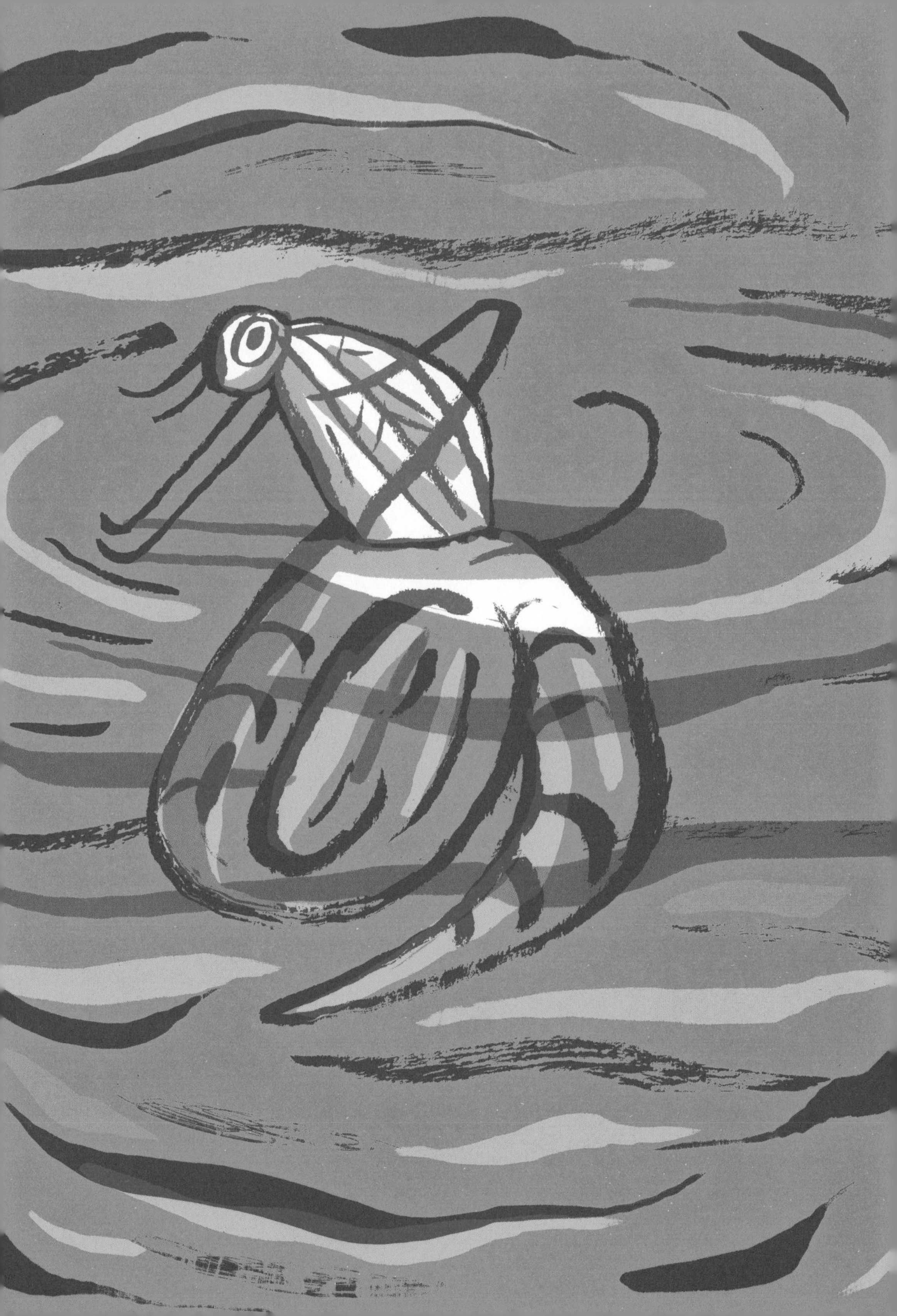

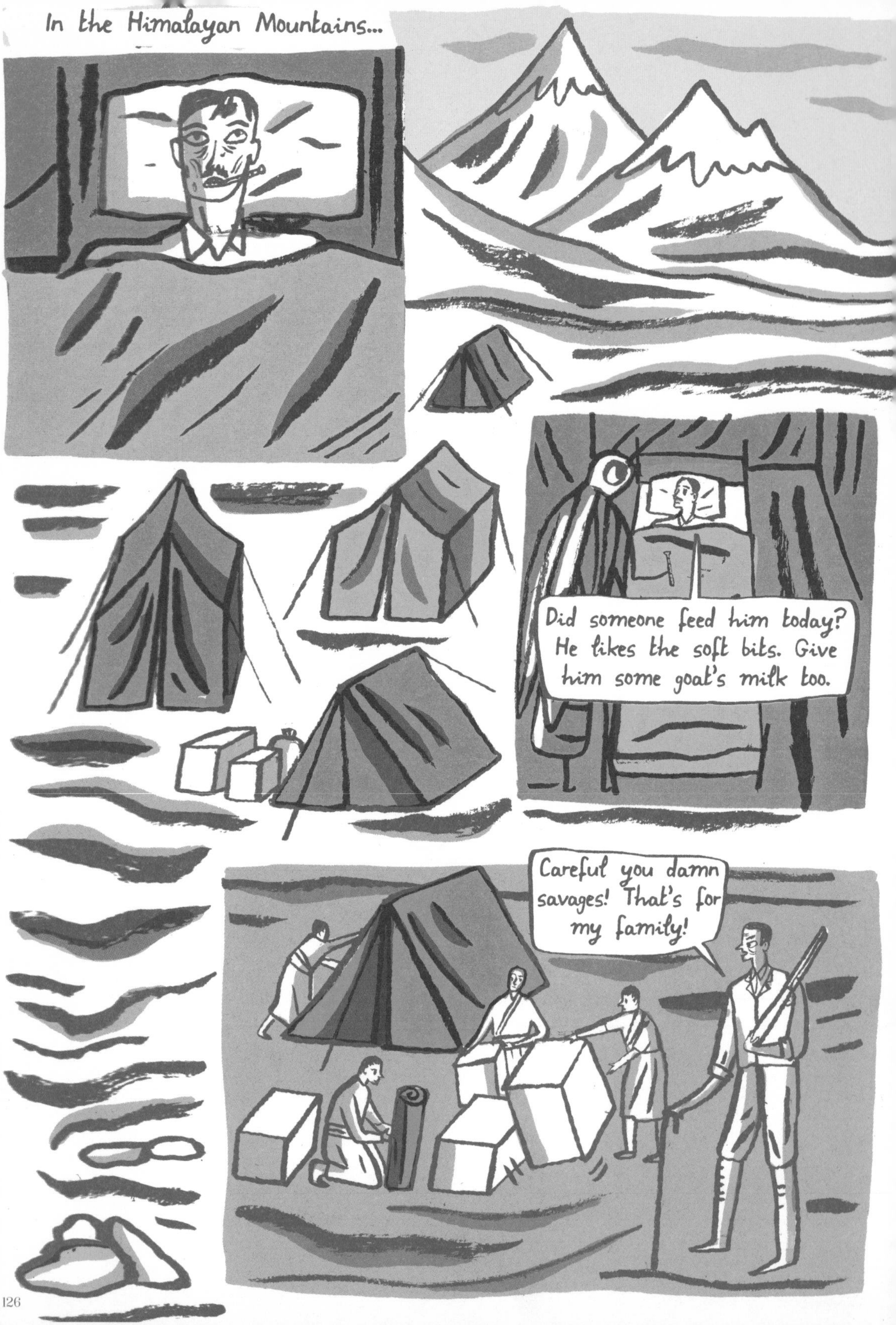
In the Himalayan Mountains...
Did someone feed him today? He likes the soft bits. Give him some goat's milk too.
Careful you damn savages! That's for my family!

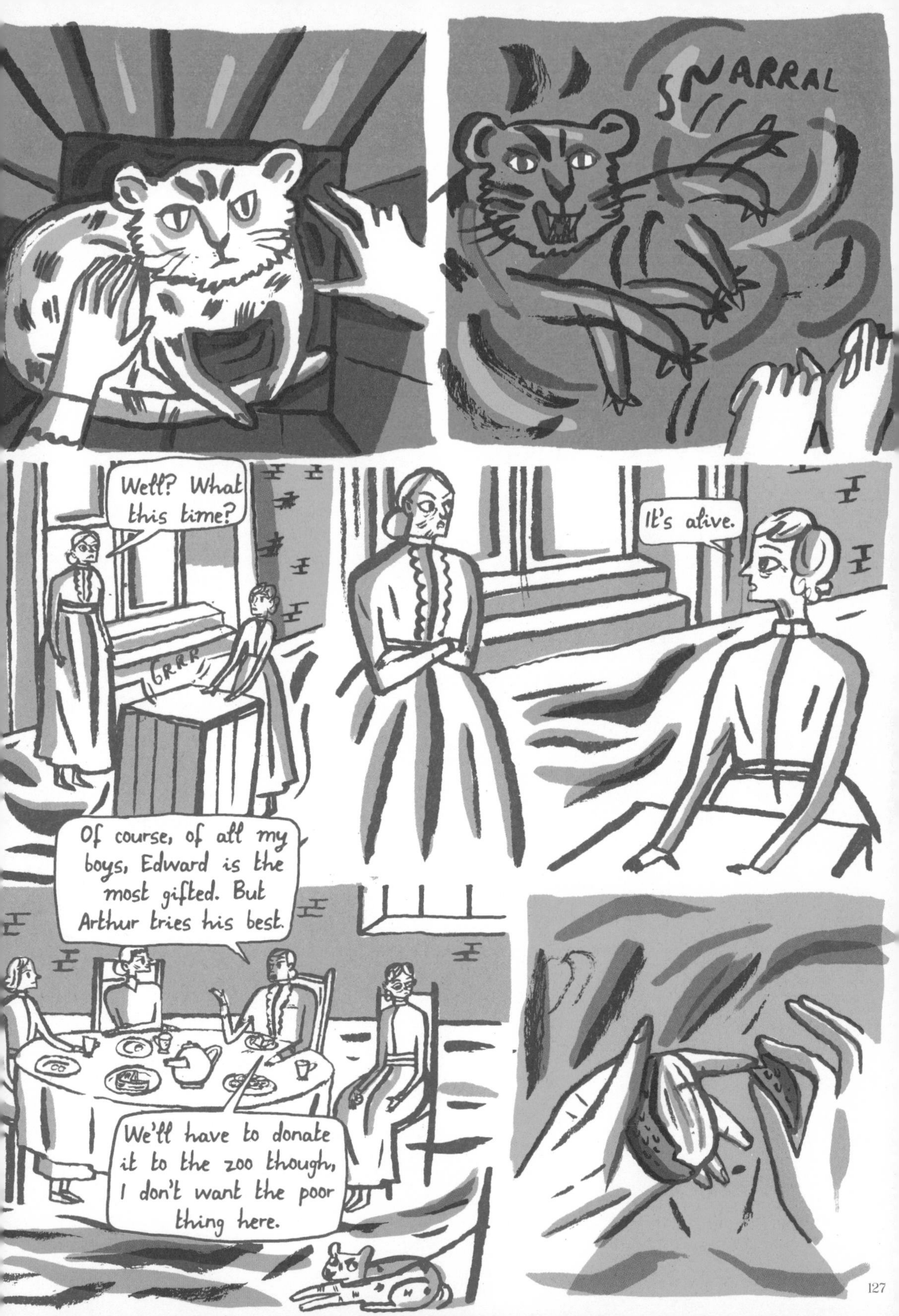
SNARRAL
Well? What this time?
GRRR
It's alive.
Of course, of all my boys, Edward is the most gifted. But Arthur tries his best.
We'll have to donate it to the zoo though, I don't want the poor thing here.

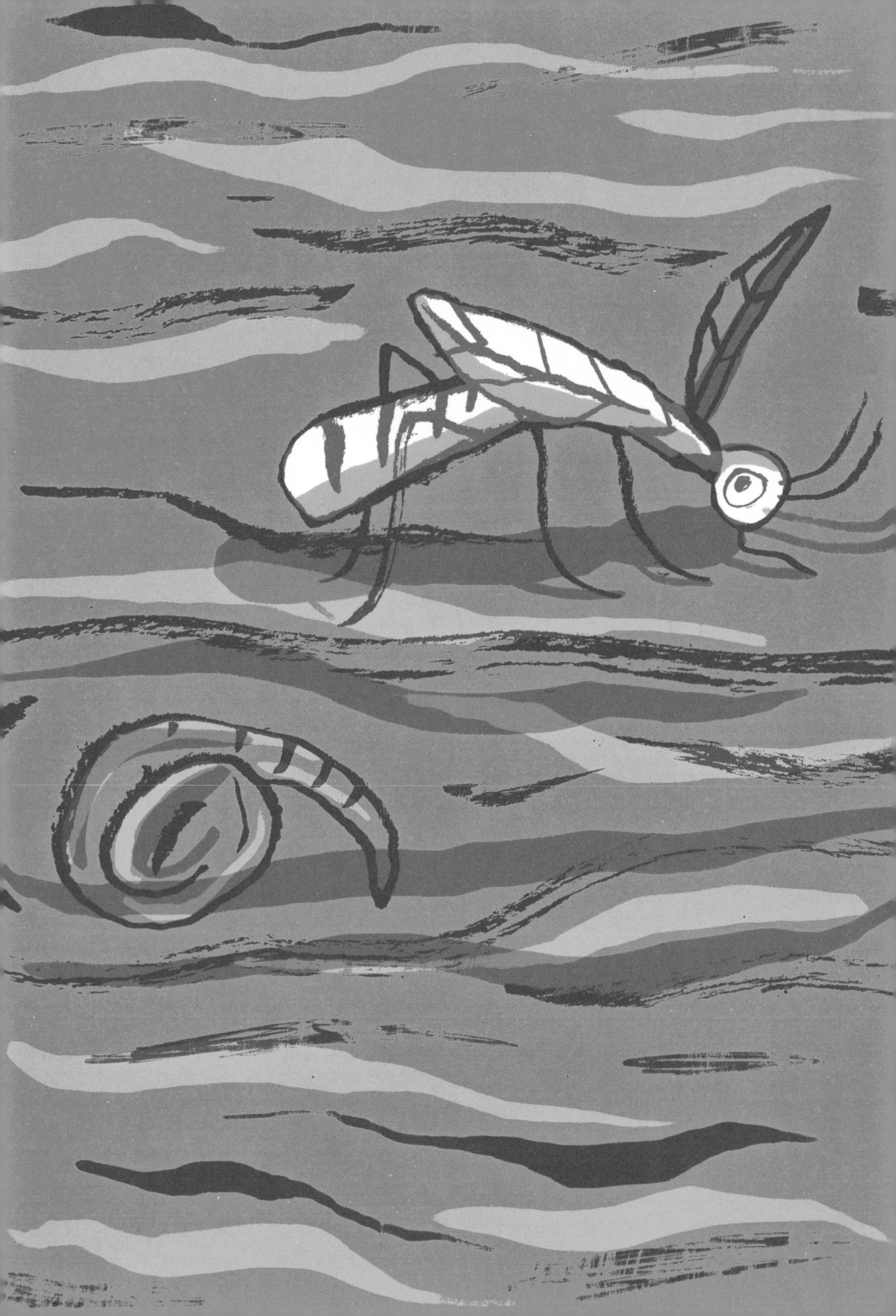

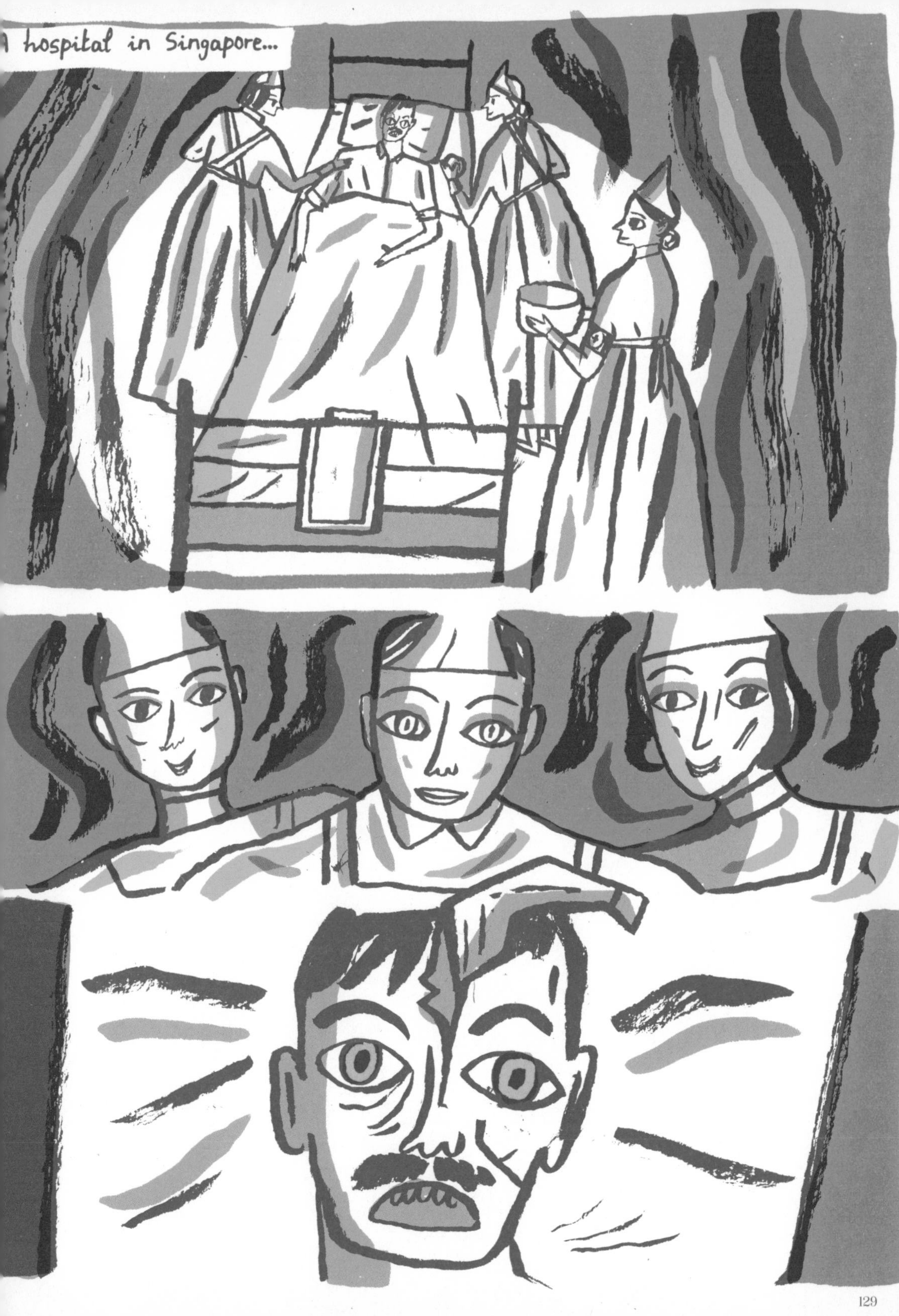
A hospital in Singapore...

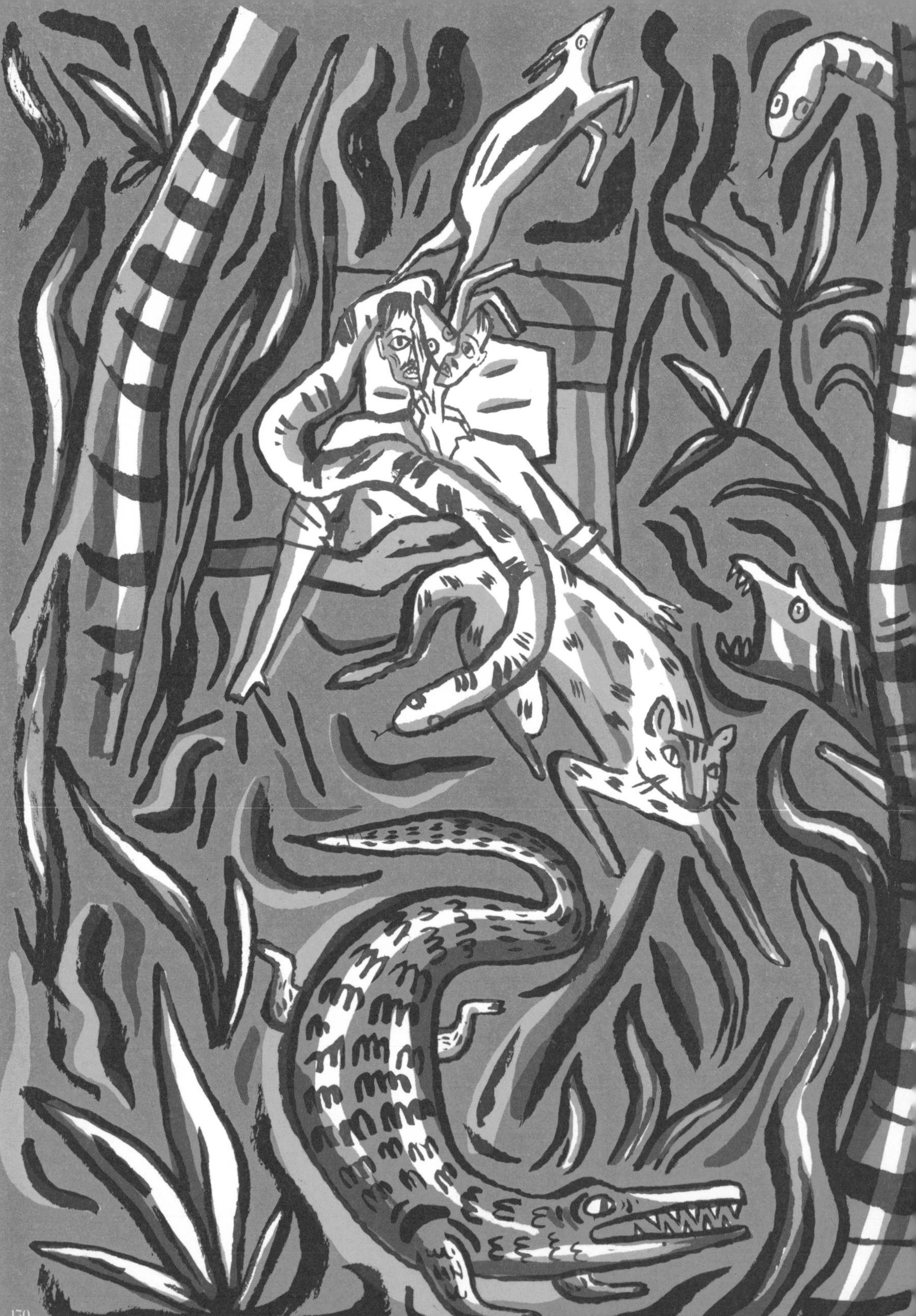

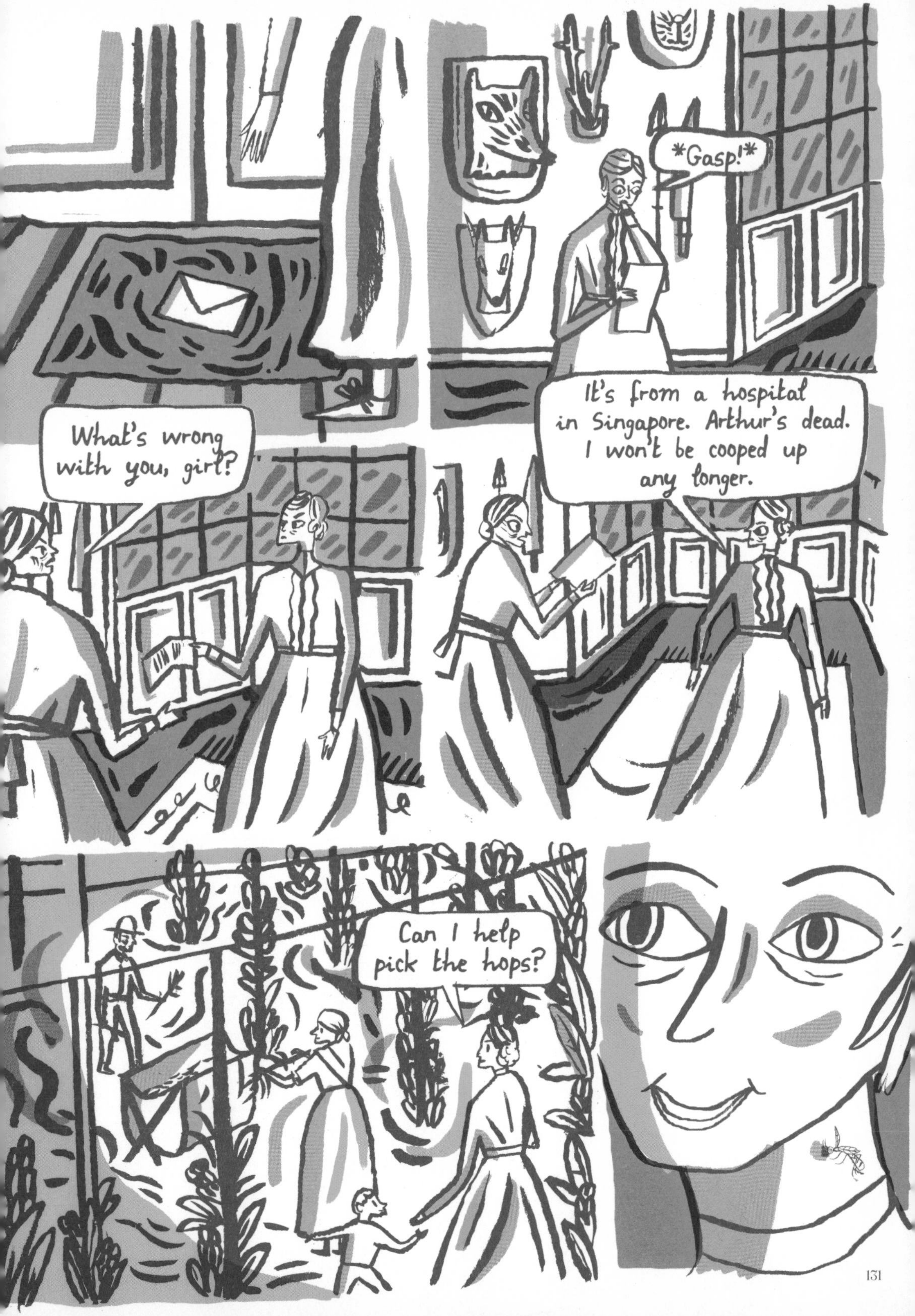
Gasp!
What's wrong with you, girl?
It's from a hospital in Singapore. Arthur's dead. I won't be cooped up any longer.
Can I help pick the hops?

The Hunter

Historical Context

1. In the Edwardian era there was a huge difference in the lives of the rich and poor, with social classes very rigidly defined. However, within the bounds of these classes, there was widespread relative prosperity. Britain was at its most powerful in economic terms, with London being the financial centre of the world.

2. There was a great trend for travel amongst the upper classes, and big game hunting was the sport of choice for many aristocrats both male and female. The British Empire still covered vast swathes of the world, and so an Englishman touring the Empire would likely have carried an attitude of superiority.

3. Big game hunting was a way for wealthy gentlemen to show what wonderful creatures they had encountered on their travels. Most people in Britain would never have seen such animals and with photography still in its infancy, hunting trophies were a means of bringing the exotic back to Britain. Of course, it was also a means for the upper classes to make a social statement that they could afford to travel to the far reaches of the world, and that once there they could be the dominant species wherever they roamed.

4. It is worth noting that there wasn't the same sentimentality towards animals at this time; hunting did not carry the emotional or ethical weight that we feel today. The Edwardian attitude would be comparable to how we might feel about playing a game of football; hunting was simply a sport.

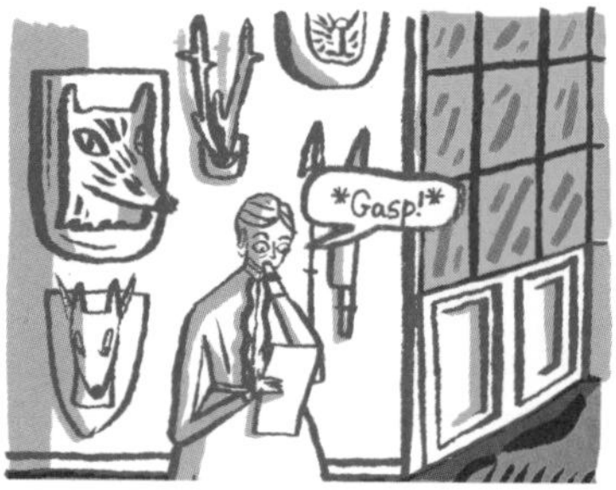
Gasp!

Factual Background
at Scotney Castle

1. The Hussey family were living in the new family mansion overlooking the old castle folly ruin. They were a very wealthy family, earlier generations having made a fortune from the Kentish iron industry, but at this time making most of their money in hops from land ownership. Kentish hops were the most valuable in the world. The Kent-Sussex border was redrawn in order to increase the number of hop fields in Kent and thus fetch the best price. Kentish hops were the world standard by which all hop prices were set.

2. In the hop season, poor families from London and other cities would take a working holiday to the castle to get some clean air and let their children play in the countryside, whilst picking hops on the castle estate to earn some extra cash.

3. There were four male children and two female children in the Hussey family at this time. The main children featured in this story are Arthur and Gertrude. Arthur was the third male in line and joined the army, travelling the world and hunting. Gertrude stayed at home for many years, eventually moving to Burwash but remaining a spinster to her death.

4. In the Hussey family archives there are lots of detailed letters, photographs and diaries from this era, including a letter from a doctor telling the family of Arthur's death of Blackwater Fever (a strain of Malaria). Arthur writes of being bitten by mosquitos in Cairo and frequently suffers bouts of sickness. There are also a number of Arthur's hunting trophies and scorecards. These collection items have inspired the story and many feature within the narrative in some way.